Things Good Mothers Know

Things Good Mothers Know

A CELEBRATION

Alexandra Stoddard

WM
WILLIAM MORROW
An Imprint of HarperCollinsPublishers

HarperCollins books may be purchased for educational, business, or sales promotional use. For information, please write: Special Markets Department, HarperCollins Publishers, 10 East 53rd Street, New York, NY 10022.

FIRST EDITION

Designed by Ashley Halsey

Library of Congress Cataloging-in-Publication Data

Stoddard, Alexandra.
   Things good mothers know: a celebration/Alexandra Stoddard.—1st ed.
      p. cm.
  ISBN-13: 978-0-06-171442-9
  ISBN-10: 0-06-171442-9
  1. Mothers. 2. Motherhood. I. Title.
  HQ759.S696 2009
  306.874'3—dc22

                                    2008040580

12 13 ◆/RRD 10 9 8 7 6 5 4 3 2

To my mother, Barbara, I am grateful to you for bringing me into this world.
Thank you for your guidance and strength.
To my two daughters, Alexandra and Brooke.
It is an honor and the greatest blessing of my life to be your mother.
And to my four precious grandchildren, Nicholas, Anna,
Lily, and Cooper, who fill my heart with continuous joy.
All my love to each of you.

Acknowledgments

Carl Brandt, my literary agent and friend, thank you for your thoughtful advice, encouragement, and support for almost fifty years, and for always knowing how to stretch me even further. "This is" as you have told me so often "the way it should be." And, thankfully, this is the way it is.

Great love to you,
Sandie

Toni Sciarra, my friend and editor of thirteen of my books, deep appreciation for your dedication to my work, your brilliant perceptions, and editing genius. I have complete trust in your judgment. Your great skill always clarifies and enhances the work. Thank you for our illuminating conversations and the joy in the process.

Great love to you,
Alexandra

My deepest thanks to all the mothers, sons, and daughters I interviewed; your wisdom and insights have informed and deepened my thinking in tangible and intangible ways.

Love and affection,
Alexandra Stoddard

To put the world in order,
we must first put the nation in order;
to put the nation in order, we must first
put the family in order; to put the family
in order, we must first cultivate our personal
life; we must first set our hearts right.

—Confucius

Contents

TWENTY YEARS FROM NOW YOU WILL BE MORE DISAPPOINTED
BY THE THINGS YOU DIDN'T DO THAN BY THE ONES YOU DID DO.
SO THROW OFF THE BOWLINES, SAIL AWAY FROM THE SAFE
HARBOR. CATCH THE TRADE WINDS IN YOUR SAILS.
EXPLORE. DREAM. DISCOVER.

—*Mark Twain*

Introduction

I'm honored to write about mothers because I feel becoming a mother was the greatest gift in my life. If I were not a mother, I would find meaning and purpose in some other way, but being the mother of two remarkable women gives me a sense of wholeness, great meaning, and satisfaction.

Before I began to write *Things Good Mothers Know*, I interviewed mothers and children of all ages. I asked searching questions and heard the most remarkable stories. Every person confirmed what I already felt—our relationships with our mothers are the most important relationships in our lives. One woman cried as she confessed that she felt she could never love or appreciate her mother enough for carrying her in her womb and giving birth to her. This exemplifies the mystery of life and love between mother and child.

As I write this, I remember my mother and the nearly forty years we were together before she died of cancer, and how much I love her. But I also think how sorry I am that she was unfulfilled in her thirty-year marriage, and how frustrated she seemed to be in general. I don't judge my mother for her choices, but I'm convinced that if she had focused more on finding her own meaning and purpose outside her children, things could have worked out better for her. The good life seemed always just beyond her reach. My mother did the best she could, and that is all anyone can expect from another person. I never felt a lack of love from her. I dedicated my book *Living a Beautiful Life* to my mother, who continues to be an extraordinary role model for teaching me why beauty is important in our daily lives. My mother was a strong, good woman who wasn't always lucky. My empathy, compassion, and love for her grow deeper year after year.

My daughters, Alexandra and Brooke, had wonderful times with my mother, and knowing this brings me great joy. As a grandmother she loosened up and became playful as she enjoyed herself without the responsibilities that are central to being a mother.

Without her own self-expression, a mother can become needy rather than resourceful. The mother who pursues her own talents, who challenges herself to greater personal excellence, who lives the good life, and who has achieved personal happiness becomes an ideal example of personal responsibility to her child. A mother's job is to encourage independence, confidence, and individual happiness. Mothers can do this by their own example of loving and letting go.

A good mother's motivations are pure: all she really wants for her child is that he or she live a satisfying, productive, happy life, while being in a position to help others to do the same. Her own striving for excellence is the core principle that will lead her to be useful and inspire others on their own paths.

Don't think if you are a good mother you will be happy. Be happy and you will be good at everything that is meaningful and valuable in your life. Raising a child to become a good person is a most honorable goal, and attaining it begins with a mother's own inner transformation.

I celebrate all mothers as they guide and shape children into flourishing adults and make lasting contributions to the world through the achievement of their own happiness.

Alexandra Stoddard

Stonington Village, Connecticut

Things Good Mothers Know

1

The Ideal Mother?

THE ONE ESSENTIAL THING IS THAT WE STRIVE TO HAVE
LIGHT IN OURSELVES. OUR STRIVINGS WILL BE RECOGNIZED
BY OTHERS AND WHEN PEOPLE HAVE LIGHT IN
THEMSELVES IT WILL SHINE OUT FROM THEM.

—*Albert Schweitzer*

I believe that mothers, at their best, try to live up to their own potential and expect their children to do the same. Each one of us was born of a mother who was also born of a mother, as her mother was, going back to the beginning of human life. Mothers affect all people on earth. What is the ideal message from these sacred messengers? Mothers embody the ultimate good, the transcendent power of true love—you deeply care for the well-being of yourself and others who often are in need of our affection and care.

No one can teach inner peace, joy, and fulfillment who doesn't embody them. Being an ideal mother means being, as much as possible, an ideal person. A mother must pay attention to herself in order to be in a position to serve others.

How can each of us—mother and child, grandmother, great-grandmother—grow to become a better human being? There has to be a balance between giving to others and nourishing our mental, physical, and spiritual selves. The ideal mother is, after all, an ordinary human being who is becoming a good person. Wise mothers grow to understand that developing their own core identity is indispensable in being a positive influence on their children.

What are the characteristics of the ideal mother? Who are some of the women you know and love who exemplify admirable qualities listed below? Here are some of the qualities I think of when I complete the sentence: The ideal mother is _____.

Happy	Grateful	Compassionate
Balanced	Authentic	Sensitive
Gentle	Dedicated	Focused
Kind	Passionate	Polite
Loving	Appropriate	Present
Caring	Creative	Adventurous
Forgiving	Honest	Reliable
Strong	Humorous	Devoted
Conscientious	Tender	Intuitive
Understanding	Patient	Humble
Generous	Wise	Encouraging

Organized	Hopeful	Fun
Inventive	Open-minded	Responsible
Philosophical	Inspiring	Energetic
Contemplative	Thoughtful	Imaginative
Enthusiastic	Optimistic	Rational
Practical	Disciplined	

Looking at this list of fifty qualities, we quickly realize these characteristics embody the principles to live by in order to become an ideal human being. No one is perfect, though we are all perfect in potential. The good news is, the more we aspire to greatness, the better our chances of achieving it. Most mothers aspire to be better people, and as a direct result, better mothers. All the mothers I interviewed wanted their sons and daughters to grow up to be good men and women. A mother who aspires to have a happy child must set an example of what happiness looks and feels like. As we grow into our potential excellence, we, in turn, are better mothers.

As much as I respect the enlightenment of the Buddha, he left his wife and child in the middle of the night to pursue his inner search. But mothers can't leave. Mothers must pursue wisdom at home, in their daily lives, at the kitchen table. Mothers have endless distractions, are constantly interrupted, and have to drop everything in an emergency. We live in the trenches of life, without the luxury of a mountaintop retreat. But when our motivation is pure, our children will survive even if we sometimes worry, are stressed, and overreact from time to time. Children raised with the right values will survive, and most will thrive when they feel personally responsible for their own inner transformation and are not focused on their so-called entitlements and rights.

Some children would rather blame their mothers than do the necessary inner work to become happy. Some mothers would rather blame their children and the demands of motherhood than make the time and effort to pursue personal fulfillment. Mothers, as we all know, can't give something they don't possess. Mothers need to practice what they preach. Children see and feel their mother's energy 24/7. A mother can't tell a child not to be grumpy and be grumpy herself. She can't teach her child to "love thy neighbor as thyself" or "do unto others as you would have them do unto you" if she is cruel to her former husband. Right thought leads to right action: what's good for you and for others.

A mother teaches her child life's most valuable lessons by never selling herself short. Mothers should establish house rules that teach the core values of being true to one's self and living an ethical life focused on love, altruism, compassion, kindness, and charity. Whether a mother agrees or disagrees with her child, she respects her child's right to have a different point of view, thus supporting diversity of human differences. Good mothers want their children to become independent thinkers. Good mothers understand the divergent paths their children may take to claim their own truth.

Mothers, we'd like to think, are practically perfect, but as we all know firsthand, there's always room for improvement. The journey to perfection is full of exciting discoveries. Blessings to you as you find new ways to let your light shine.

IT IS A PARADOXICAL BUT PROFOUNDLY TRUE
AND IMPORTANT PRINCIPLE OF LIFE THAT THE
MOST LIKELY WAY TO REACH A GOAL IS TO BE AIMING
NOT AT THE GOAL ITSELF BUT AT SOME
MORE AMBITIOUS GOAL BEYOND IT.

—*Arnold Toynbee*

2

Life Changes but Love Does Not

LOVE IS NOT LOVE WHICH ALTERS
WHEN IT ALTERATION FINDS . . .

—Shakespeare

Good mothers know never to withhold their love from a child no matter what the circumstances. Love is the legacy that is eternal.

In *Letters to a Young Poet*, Rainer Maria Rilke teaches us about love: "This is the miracle that happens every time to those who really love: the more they give, the more they possess of that preciously nourishing love form." One young mother told me as she wiped away some tears that she never knew she could love so deeply until she gave birth to her daughter. We open our hearts wider, broader, and deeper in this self-generating goodness of pure love. The Greek dramatist Euripides knew that "love is all we have, the only way that each can help the other."

When love is mutual, we look up to each other with no consideration of age or rank. I feel the miracle of being given the extraordinary opportunity to be the mother of Alexandra and Brooke. I look up to them and always have, and our shared respect sustains us in our relationship as adults. I have always put them first when they needed me, and they literally taught me about the true nature of love.

A loveable mother is such a resource to her child. A kiss on a boo-boo from a tender, loving mama makes the pain go away and a child can run back to the sandbox and continue to play. When love is always available, children grow up to be confident adults ready to take on the world, believing in giving and receiving love. Good mothers know that love does make the world go around.

Love should not expect anything in return. When we are illuminated by love, we feel great joy. I often say that none of us will ever know how much others love and cherish us, and even without that knowledge our life is shaped by the power of our own love reaching out toward others. Love gives generously and happiness lies in the thoughtful act of loving.

Pure love is never needy. The more love we generate, the greater our capacity to spread it in dark corners of the planet. The French Romantic writer Gustave Flaubert believed that "love is a springtime plant that perfumes everything with hope." It is quite fascinating to see how love operates in action. It is no longer about me, it is about you. And you and you.

Many mothers confided to me that they have unhappy children. Even a child raised in a loving environment sometimes suffers, and we feel sadness when someone we dearly love is unhappy. Many grown children told me of their unhappy mothers. When we love wholeheartedly, we feel others' pain, but there is nothing in the world we can do for them but be more loving. And because we never know how powerful our love can be to someone, we can be confident that love is all a person needs even when not receptive to it. The American Trappist monk and writer Thomas Merton put this truth best when he wrote, "One must face the terrible responsibility of the decision to love in spite of all unworthiness whether in oneself or in one's neighbor."

Peter, my husband, soul mate, and best friend believes love gives and serves without hesitation. I heard an expression from a friend of a friend: "You've got to love the crusts." When I inquired what that meant, a major life lesson was presented to me: if we cut the crusts off a sandwich, the way we do when we make everything "perfect" for our children, they may be robbed of the best nutrients of the bread. When we love, we love without restrictions and we don't judge. We love another as he is, not as he could be or should be. I've grown to believe that love is the only way to be of service to others. If I'm ever less than my happy self, I realize it is because I'm not being loving enough. When I love someone as much as myself, and when I love myself as much as I love others, I'm happy as a result.

Love tenderly. Love gently. Khalil Gibran wrote in his classic book *The Prophet*, "Wake at dawn with a winged heart and give thanks for another day of loving." Be there for your loved ones. Be there for yourself. The process of living and loving makes us who we are and determines what will become of us. Love never dies. It remains in the hearts and souls of everyone who shared this amazing grace. Be the light bearer with your love. Everything, everyone, everywhere will benefit from your loving spirit, and you will be happy.

Great love to you always.

So long as we love we serve; so long
as we are loved by others, I would
almost say that we are indispensable.

—*Robert Louis Stevenson*

3

Simplicity: The New Luxury

CULTIVATE SIMPLICITY.

—Charles Lamb

Gradually we are beginning to appreciate the integrity of simplicity. Albert Einstein instructs, "Everything should be made as simple as possible, but not simpler." How true, but how few of us understand the joy of true, pure simplicity? It seems that in order to appreciate the luxury of simplicity, we first need to crowd our lives with things and with obligations that accumulate until we feel a bit overwhelmed. Slowly, we learn to let go of some of our baggage and grow into an awareness that simplicity makes us happy: simple things make us feel good.

Great minds know how to distill the divine essence of their work by stripping away excess. The great sculptor knows that the block of marble is just a huge block of marble until Michelangelo chips the extraneous away, revealing a simply magnificent work of art. The artist applies wisdom and skill to arrive at what is not too fancy or too plain but what is disarmingly simple and just right in its powerful beauty. We are lifted up by the artful elegance of this simplicity and beauty.

Simplicity and luxury seem to be opposites, but if you've ever had the luxury of a weekend when you have no plans and are free to do whatever feels right at the moment, you understand the luxury of simplicity.

Good mothers know that families need the luxury of unstructured time together, when they can decide at the last minute what would be fun to do. Children just want to be with you. You don't have to be doing anything spectacular. Being parents who give undivided attention, listen well, ask questions, and put their children first is a luxury for the child. There is no scheduled party, just time together. If your son is playing in a softball game that conflicts with an important meeting, show up at his game, late if necessary, but show up. Turn off your cell phone and give him your full attention. This way you're doing your best, even though you had to juggle things, and in the car on the way home you can intelligently, lovingly discuss the game and your son's participation.

What simple luxuries do you appreciate? These may vary from year to year, from time to time, so it's wise to periodically redefine them. Some luxuries may be lovely, but not simple. If you love to surf, first you have to get to a beach with energetic waves. If you enjoy skiing, you need to be where there is snow and mountains. Enjoyable? Yes. Simple? Not necessarily. When I was doing interior design work, I made all my decisions based on a triangle of simplicity, appropriateness, and beauty. I've found that this theory can be applied to our daily lives.

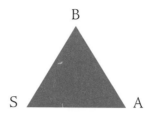

What is simple and appropriate is beautiful. A chicken put in a crock-pot in the morning that results in a home-cooked supper that evening with no fuss and bother qualifies on all counts.

Appropriate choices are based on reality. Wise people live within their means and save for a rainy day. Everyone who is living responsibly should have some cash set aside for emergencies or contingencies. Be clear that your decisions are fitting to your circumstances.

At the top of the triangle is beauty. Think of the beauty of a smile, a love pat, a kiss. Consider the simple luxury of allowing a few extra minutes in the morning to get the children up, dressed, and fed. Mornings can become a pleasant ritual rather than a frantic race.

Make a list of some of your experiences that were luxuriously simple. Here are some of mine:

- *Eating bouillabaisse in a terrace garden with dear friends, sipping wine, enjoying good conversation and laughter*
- *Having a massage by the water's edge*
- *Taking a shower after an ocean swim*
- *Sleeping on a sleeping porch*
- *Enjoying meals outside*

- *Having a view of my garden from the kitchen sink*
- *Having a picnic with my grandchildren*

Think of the houses where you feel the most comfortable and the places where you like to vacation. What elements can you bring into your life to add simple luxury? When we simplify our style, our houses feel comfortable. An uncluttered, Zen-calm space is a spa to the soul. Impressionist painter Claude Monet's house in Giverny is surprisingly simple and endearing in its hominess. All the furniture in the dining room, for example, is simply painted a cheerful yellow. Lao-Tzu warns, "To have little is to possess: to have plenty is to be perplexed." He urges us to "manifest plainness, embrace simplicity, reduce selfishness, have few desires."

Leonardo da Vinci believed in the power of simplicity to refine our minds: "Small rooms or dwellings discipline the mind; large ones weaken it." Last year while we were renovating our cottage, Peter and I spent several months living at the Inn at Stonington, the enchanting place where we host our Happiness Weekends and our Writer's Happiness Retreat. We lived in one small room and found it delightful. We had each other, our work, books, flowers, and our inner resources.

Simplicity requires self-confidence and self-awareness. Do you prefer a terra-cotta pot to a decorated cachepot? Do you prefer a simple roasted chicken to a dish with heavy sauces? When you know what you want, life becomes much simpler. Simplify your life with no apologies. You have nothing to prove to anyone but yourself. A beautiful life well lived is the new luxury.

THERE IS NO GREATNESS
WHERE THERE IS NOT SIMPLICITY,
GOODNESS, AND TRUTH.

—Leo Tolstoy

4

Redefine Perfectionism: Experience Excellence Now

IF HAPPINESS IS ACTIVITY IN ACCORDANCE
WITH EXCELLENCE, IT IS REASONABLE THAT
IT SHOULD BE IN ACCORDANCE WITH THE
HIGHEST EXCELLENCE.

—*Aristotle*

I believe that perfectionism—striving to be perfect and expecting the same of others—is the root of many of our troubles. Many of the mothers I interviewed admitted to suffering from this tyranny that offers no relief. Perfectionism should not be confused with idealism. Perfection is rooted in hubris, the arrogance of thinking that one's own way is the only right way. Perfectionists view everything—their children, their spouses, their houses, their gardens, their friends, their careers—as extensions of themselves. In so doing, they shoulder unnecessary burdens at a deep cost to themselves and others.

Perfectionism stifles creativity and resourcefulness. We become terrified of making a mistake even though we know that geniuses such as Albert Einstein failed more often than they succeeded. How dreadful to render ourselves powerless before we begin anything big and important. How liberating to connect with our passion and not get stuck in creating something that is flawless; instead, we can just show up regularly and do our best.

Good mothers resist getting bogged down in details, otherwise they would have no time or energy to accomplish anything but the mundane. I've learned to ease up on things that aren't of any real importance. Who cares about having perfect hair if it keeps you from swimming with your children? I have friends who won't host dinner parties because everything has to be perfect. They literally make themselves sick over their elaborate efforts, yet we'd all rather sit around a kitchen table enjoying pasta and Pinot Grigio, sharing laughs and conversation. Wouldn't such gatherings set a positive example for our children?

Renoir's painting *Luncheon of the Boating Party* reminds me to celebrate love and friendship spontaneously, complete with elbows on the table and a puppy, also on (not at) the table, embraced by his mistress. Wrinkles and crumbs are an integral part of authentic experience.

Since perfection is unattainable in this world, I vote we bury it and move on to enjoying ourselves and our time with our children and friends. When we liberate ourselves from the prison of perfection, we can experience excellence now. Right where you are is an opportunity to excel, to be and become better at whatever you put your mind and hand to. Our job is to find a wide variety of ways to use as much of our potential as possible, to raise our consciousness as high and deep and broad as we can. When we do, we feel exhilaration, balance, and freedom. Particularly with all the demands of raising children, we mothers have to always remember who we are.

When we accept the challenge of personal growth, we will be less demanding of our children, because we will be more understanding of both their limitations and their great, varied gifts. Our children are not perfect, either, but they have great potential. By concentrating on our potential more than on perfection, we see that our capacity for growth is vast.

Peter F. Drucker, a best-selling author on management, wisely notes, "There is nothing so useless as doing efficiently that which should not be done at all." When we focus on things that are significant, that bring us joy and satisfaction, we become one with our pursuits and feel relaxed and content rather than frustrated and stressed. Let's raise the bar higher, always trying to experience excellence—not perfection—now.

The Constitution of the United States did not propose a "perfect" Union, but "a more perfect" Union. Make the pursuit of excellence your "more perfect" goal. Make a list of ways you can experience excellence now.

- *Go the extra mile in focused effort, but take breaks and let yourself do your best without berating yourself for not doing something perfectly.*
- *Understand that mental, moral, and spiritual excellence is your*

lasting contribution to the world and your example will be modeled in future generations.

· *Admit your limitations and accept them in others. No one is excellent in every area of life. Strive to be well rounded inwardly in balance to your outer accomplishments.*

· *Value excellent relationships with others that are based on love, respect, and kindness. Shakespeare wrote: "Kind is my love today, tomorrow kind, Still constant in a wondrous excellence."*

· *Accept that there is always room for improvement. Keep working with the ordinary and notch it toward superiority.*

· *Continuously question whether you are concentrating too much on minutia that rob you of pursuing excellence. Be less critical of small matters.*

· *Remember that our lives are far from perfect, but when we take the pieces we have and make the best of them, we do pretty well.*

Rather than desiring perfection, let us instead desire excellence. Excellence, to my mind, *is* perfect.

DEAD PERFECTION, NO MORE.

—*Alfred, Lord Tennyson*

5

Know When to Say No

MEN MUST BE DECIDED ON WHAT THEY WILL
NOT DO, AND THEN THEY ARE ABLE TO ACT WITH
VIGOR IN WHAT THEY OUGHT TO DO.

—*Mencius*

Good mothers know when to say no in order to give to others from a loving heart. Whenever we go beyond our capacity to spaciously love and thrive, everyone and everything suffers. We need time and space to renew ourselves, free of the endless demands of others, or we will become overextended and resentful.

Children did not ask to be born. Since they're not here voluntarily, it's our responsibility to make sure their time spent here with us is enjoyable and uplifting. No mother can be available to anyone, no matter what the circumstances, without regular breaks.

After interviewing my oldest daughter, Alexandra, then three, for admission to day school, the head of the school instructed me that she was ready to leave the nest a bit and spend time with her peers. I was a working mother and must have expressed some guilt about not being a full-time mother. This wonderful educator reached across the desk, touched my arm, and said, "Alexandra, your daughter won't break without you." A great sense of relief enveloped me.

We must say no to smothering our children. The poem written by Guillaume Apollinaire applies: "'Come to the edge.' 'We can't. We're afraid.' 'Come to the edge.' 'We can't. We will fall!' 'Come to the edge.' And they came. And he pushed them. And they flew." This encouragement is not a refusal to be a loving caregiver; there must be a balance between give and take in all relationships. If we neglect our own needs, we snuff out our inner light and expansiveness. Good mothers need deep reserves of patience, tolerance, understanding, and perseverance. We're in this bond for life. We cannot do it if we overdo.

I've always understood my need to say no to the pressures of others, even if I felt awkward in doing so. I'm not always ready to inquire, "What can I do for you?" When I ask this question, I'm full of gratitude to be in a position to be of use. When I'm hopelessly behind in my work, I say no to invitations. I turn down opportunities: "I'm sorry, but the timing isn't right." I refuse to live on automatic pilot, jumping from one thing to another.

The busier the mother, the greater the need for regular breaks. Rather than getting caught in the "second shift" role of home chores on top of work responsibilities, we need to free ourselves from everyone and everything several times a day in order to dependably be a loving, sustaining presence. How you do this will vary, depending your life circumstances. When your children are small, read while they nap—say no to chores, work, or phone calls. When they're in school, take some time for yourself. We are not victims of our circumstances; we create them. With careful organization and self-knowledge we can nurture ourselves in equal measure to the loving kindness we give.

Children want what they want and they want it now. It's not their job to take care of us. We are not born understanding that it is better to give than to receive. This wisdom is taught by adults. Good mothers do not comply with the wishes of others if they are not appropriate or reasonable. We say yes on our own terms and no when that is the proper choice. No one, including our children, should have the power to control us.

Unless we maintain a Zen-calm balance in our lives, we will say things we'll regret and do things that are unloving. Children should not be exposed to the improper behavior of their caregivers. We must say no to acting in negative, inappropriate ways. "Do not allow yourself," Marcus Aurelius warned, "to be infected by the mood or spirit of those who abuse you; do not step into their path." We continuously decide how to best act in the circumstances we find ourselves in, in order to do the right thing to the best of our ability.

My husband Peter Brown believes that saying NO to someone means saying YES to someone else. We have to be exceedingly careful how we spend our precious time on this short earthly journey. Whenever we say yes to someone, we should try to be at our best; then yes will be the right choice: good for us and for others.

FORMULA OF MY HAPPINESS: A YES,
A NO, A STRAIGHT LINE, A GOAL.

—*Nietzsche*

6

Maintenance: A Blessing or a Burden?

MANY WEALTHY PEOPLE
ARE LITTLE MORE THAN THE
JANITORS OF THEIR POSSESSIONS.

—*Frank Lloyd Wright*

What possessions do you deeply treasure? What are the objects of your affection? Without looking around your home, make a list of all the things you truly love in your daily life. Now put them into categories:

- *Clothes*
- *Art*
- *Furniture*

- *Accessories*
- *House*
- *Pets or animals*
- *Garden and yard*
- *Car*
- *Appliances and gadgets*

As good mothers, we know that our children are our highest priority and require the most maintenance. And with children we need more space, bigger houses, larger lawns, and increasing maintenance. After allowing for your family's immediate needs and wants, how do you honestly feel about the possessions you own? Now that you have listed and categorized them, ask yourself: do you feel you have acquired too much of a good thing? Are you willing to maintain these objects even if they crowd your space? Do they give you daily enjoyment? Are you willing to spend time, energy, and money to protect and care for them? Do you ever feel burdened by the quantity of your favorite things and feel you have too much "stuff" around?

Do you believe the maintenance of your lifestyle is a blessing or a burden? Years ago, our daughter Alexandra told us she believes 90 percent of life is maintenance. That figure seemed high to me, but now I agree. Everything we have is our responsibility to maintain, to keep alive, to keep in good repair. Maintenance comes from the Latin, *manu tenere*—to hold in the hand. What we own is in our hands.

"Housekeeping," *Little Women* author Louisa May Alcott understood, "ain't no joke." When Peter and I bought a dilapidated eighteenth-century house in 1988, my friend and literary agent Carl

Brandt congratulated me and said, "You'll never be bored." This enchanting old cottage has needed continuous maintenance. As much as we love our house, there have definitely been, and still are, times when the blessing becomes a burden.

In 2006 we decided enough was enough and put our house on the market. After replacing the roof and all of the wood gutters, we felt it was time to pass our sweet house on to people with young children who would need the space. No one bought our house. The housing market was going into a serious slump. We've decided to live full-time in our cottage, and we are making adjustments to have less stuff around so we can enjoy our spaces with less in them to maintain.

What things do you really need to make your life satisfying? I suggest you make two lists. The first list, *Things I Love to Care For*, should contain all your material blessings—the objects you love to feed, clothe, shelter, dust, vacuum, scrub, fluff, sweep, paint, clean, water, arrange, prune, polish, wash, fold, and iron. I find my list is on the short side! I love having beautiful objects, but my interest in maintaining them is not strong. If we don't choose to maintain our own lifestyle, we need to hire people to help us—we become the maintainers of those who help us maintain.

Make another list of *Things I Don't Love to Care For*. My list is quite long. I've made a new habit of living more lightly, and I love the freedom it brings.

Growing children require more than enough maintenance. Be realistic about what you will gladly be responsible for and what you're willing to delegate or discard. I enjoy polished silver and brass, but I'm not always in the mood to be the polisher. My daughters love caring for their plants, trees, and flowers. I adore the roses that hug the picket fence, and caring for them brings joy. Our daughter Alexandra is happiest caring for and loving her dog.

There is a great deal of maintenance in our lives, especially in the lives of mothers. Let us select carefully what we willingly choose to take care of, and then count our blessings.

A MAN BUILDS A FINE HOUSE; AND NOW
HE HAS A MASTER, AND A TASK FOR LIFE:
HE IS TO FURNISH, WATCH, SHOW IT, AND
KEEP IT IN REPAIR, THE REST OF HIS DAYS.

—*Emerson*

7

Let Go of Fear

When I learned that a friend from Florida was coming to our writer's conference, I inquired if she was bringing her brilliant, well-read neighbor who is writing a book. "Oh, no," Sharon explained, "Jill never leaves the house. She's afraid." "Afraid of what?" I inquired. "Everything," Sharon quietly responded.

Good mothers are driven by love, not fear. Fear is never okay, because it defeats joy. I believe that the biggest shift in consciousness we must make post–9/11 is to realize we must teach our children not to be fearful. The actions of enlightened people are not fear-based.

If a mother frequently exhibits agitation, her children sense her apprehension and develop a habit of fearfulness. This is a heavy burden to pass on to a child. Be it claustrophobia, fear of heights, fear of cancer, fear of death, or fear of someone breaking into your house, fear is disabling and prevents you from enthusiastically moving forward with your life.

Be not afraid. All will be well. Whenever I speak to high school students, I tell them, "Always remember your brilliance," reminding them they are the hope for a peaceful, happy future. They complain that their teachers and parents lecture them about avoiding all the "wrong" behaviors rather than reinforcing their goodness, their excellence.

The American author Katherine Mansfield died of tuberculosis at age thirty-five. "Risk! Risk anything!" she cries out. "Do the hardest thing on earth for you. Act for yourself. Face the truth." When I ask someone, "What is the worst thing that could happen?" the reply is either "I'm going to die" or "something awful might happen to my child." Well, the truth is we are going to die, and if something dreadful does happen to our child, we must trust that we will have the strength to deal with it. Fearing the worst only saps our resources.

Katherine Mansfield has a powerful suggestion: "If you wish to live, you must first attend your own funeral." Will it be a celebration of one who dared to live with intensity and exuberance every day?

Make a list of your fears. Are they rational? What will you do if some of your fears become reality? Mark Twain wisely notes, "Courage is resistance to fear, mastery of fear—not absence of fear."

Living the good life requires courage. When we cultivate the quality of mind that enables us to face danger with resolve, we will be doing our best. Nothing more is expected of us. Everyone will face difficult situations, but I believe we should not focus on potential problems but on all the good we can do when we maintain a positive outlook and take steps to achieve the best outcome.

The Bible teaches that there is no fear in love. The more energy we put into love, the less we dwell on fear. Make a list of all that you love in life—the people, the places, and the things. Have some fun with this exercise. What brings you the greatest joy? What is life-enhancing? What best represents you at your core? Now make a second list of all the authors who have been your teachers. Next to each name, write in a few words what that author taught you. When I made my list, I realized what a sponge I am for the great minds teaching me to live without fear. Emerson taught me self-reliance. He said, "We are very near to greatness: one step and we are safe; Can we not take the leap?" The Greek historian, Thucydides, understood as Aristotle did that "happiness depends on being free, and freedom depends on being courageous." Tacitus, a Roman historian, taught, "The desire for safety stands against every great and noble enterprise."

Now make a third list: what people in your life personify an affirmative outlook? Name those good souls whose boldness you admire and want to emulate.

One constructive way to let go of fear is to write down your own affirmations and those of the authors who have helped to elevate your thinking. If you write them on 3 x 5 or 4 x 6 index cards, you can put one on your desk each day to inspire you. Today, you may choose Emerson: "Don't waste life in doubts and fears; spend yourself on the work before you, well assured that the right performance of this hour's duties will be the best preparation for the hours or ages that follow it."

None of us knows the full extent of our vast inner resources. I have never yet been overwhelmed to the point of complete defeat. When asked if I'm brave, my answer is, "I will be." I cultivate courage and optimism, not fear, and I trust that I will step up when necessary. Know that you carry strength within wherever you are, whatever may happen.

Be sensible, not fearful. Look both ways when crossing the street. Don't surf without a friend. Don't drive when you drink. Don't go out alone at night in a neighborhood you know is dangerous. Have regular medical checkups. Be sensible and careful, then be free to live.

I'm up and off on a great adventure. I don't know exactly where this journey will take me, but I want it to be full of love, light, laughter, and happiness. Fear not, and join me on this quest for the good life.

TRUE NOBILITY IS EXEMPT FROM FEAR.

—Shakespeare

8

Excess Is Destructive

IT IS IN THE MIND, AND NOT THE SUM,
THAT MAKES EVERY PERSON RICH . . .
NO ONE CAN BE POOR THAT HAS ENOUGH,
NOR RICH, THAT COVETS MORE THAN HE HAS.

—*Seneca*

Several years ago I found myself in New York City for a week after a period of nonstop travel. I was out of shape and decided I'd go to a yoga class every day. I walked the twenty blocks to class in the glorious sunshine, flowers, and budding trees of springtime. I felt on top of the world. After class I showered and walked back home. Who could ask for anything more?

In Friday's class we were asked to stand on our head. Hm. "I can do this." After all, this was my fifth two-hour class that week. I was in shape. Right?

That afternoon I gave a lecture and continued to feel terrific. Saturday morning Peter and I flew to Washington to visit the grandchildren. As I stood in our daughter's kitchen, I suddenly felt ill and everything seemed to spin around me. I was sicker than I'd ever been in my life. That evening the motion of the car made me sick. For several days I was in bed throwing up. Any movement of my head made me dizzy and nauseous. Once home, my doctor sent me to a neurologist. When the doctor asked me to stand on one leg with my hands up, I couldn't last a millisecond. The doctor told me after an examination I had a virus in my inner ear. Could it have been the air pressure on the flight to Washington that brought on the symptoms of pain and illness? I still don't know for sure.

Looking back, I realize I had an excess of energy. I came back from a yoga class and remember vigorously painting the soot on the kitchen ceiling of the apartment.

What are some of the excesses in your life? What do you feel is superfluous? Do you feel you have too much stuff? Too many clothes? Shoes? Jewelry? One mother told me she was excessively indulgent with her son, seeking his attention and love by giving him too much money and food. He became obese and almost flunked out of college, having no ambition to excel.

Parents who overindulge their children are doing themselves and their children a great disservice. This particular mother was divorced and desperately tried to have her son love her more than he loved his father. Although she believed that the money would provide enriching and educational experiences, it would have been healthier for her child to rough it more, to feel ambitious enough to earn some money on his own and not feel superior to everyone else. Instead, he became fat and lazy; certainly this was not his mother's intention.

Eliminating excesses leads to great freedom and pleasure. We are less likely to be stressed by our own behaviors: overeating and then dieting; neglecting our health to the point of requiring medication to correct illness; buying too much and developing a credit problem.

Having a beautiful house and garden can bring pleasure and beauty to us and our children, but if we want our house to be bigger and more elaborate than our neighbor's, our motive is not pure and we slip into excess and ostentation.

As an interior designer, I witnessed the dangers of excess. I had a client who loved to shop and spend money. The more expensive the object, the more she valued it. Her father had spoiled her, and she did the same to her ungrateful children. One of my assignments was to enlarge her enormous dressing room by twenty feet. This woman kept adding clothes to her wardrobe without eliminating any. She was willing to take space away from her backyard, garden, and pool area in order to add thousands more hangers and shoe racks.

A cabinetmaker I worked with believed that our closet space should be sufficient for a lifetime because we should eliminate an item when we add something. This advice makes good sense. Thrift shops and charities abound. If we want something new we should give up something old, allowing someone else to enjoy it. Emerson understood the give and take of life, and our interdependence: "Every man is a consumer and ought to be a producer."

Make a list of the areas in your life where you feel you verge on excess.

Make another list of others' excesses that irritate you. Below in no particular order is a list of excesses. Review them and make your own judgment.

- *Too much homework for a child in grade school*
- *Too much pressure on a child to excel*
- *Too-large portions of food at restaurants*
- *Unrealistic expectations*
- *The expense of a wedding*
- *Holiday gift giving*
- *The elaborate preparation, time, and expense of a dinner party*
- *Floral bouquets you don't arrange yourself*
- *Going out every night of the week*
- *Doing your children's homework*
- *Exercising to the point of chronic injury*
- *Doing too much for your children and then resenting it*
- *Not accepting your age and taking expensive, dangerous measures to try to look as young as your daughter*
- *Never bending the rules for your children*
- *Staying at home with your children at tremendous personal sacrifice and refusing to delegate anything to others willing to help*
- *Spending more time earning money than living*
- *Forcing your children to eat everything on their plates*
- *Overmedicating yourself*
- *Not letting go of your children*
- *Overindulging your children*
- *Overprogramming your children's after-school events, play dates, and weekend schedules*

- *Complaining constantly*
- *Spending time and money on hair, nails, toes, and makeup*
- *Worrying about everything*
- *Hampering enjoyment of life with too much neatness*
- *Demanding too much contact with grown children*
- *"Enforcing command performances" on all holidays*
- *Gossiping*
- *Being driven by power*
- *Clinging to rigid traditions*
- *Bragging about your accomplishments*

One way to cultivate our invisible riches is to understand what really makes us happy. When we do, we see that enough is often better than a feast because we are already at the banquet of life and can return to it every day, joyfully participating in the rich experiences that living continuously unfolds for us.

As mothers, we have a delicate balance to strike: we want to give every advantage to our children, but we don't want them to lose their drive, passion, and sense of personal accomplishment. I think there is such a thing, as the French say, as "the embarrassment of riches." Too much good flips to the opposite.

The more conscious we are about avoiding excess, the more we're able to use our inner and external resources constructively. I hope if I suffer from excess it will be in charity, kindness, compassion, gratitude, and appreciation. These we can cultivate assiduously because they will be our strength whatever the future holds.

WE DESIRE MOST WHAT WE OUGHT NOT TO HAVE.

—*Publilius Syrus*

9

Do, Don't Overdo

WE BECOME TEMPERATE BY
ABSTAINING FROM INDULGENCE,
AND WE ARE THE BETTER ABLE TO
ABSTAIN FROM INDULGENCE AFTER
WE HAVE BECOME TEMPERATE.

—Aristotle

All of us, especially mothers, should strive not to overdo. I'm all in favor of using as much of our potential as possible and I have a strong work ethic, but when we don't take breaks and unwind, our efforts become counterproductive. We become less able to absorb life's lessons and riches.

Our unique temperament, health, and experience should guide us so we don't learn the hard way not to overdo by suffering poor health, mental and emotional exhaustion, or damaged relationships. Aristotle urges us to live a life of great purpose and continuous learning; his principle of the Golden Mean flows into every aspect of life. Aristotle believed that when we do what is good for us we should take pleasure in the activity, and that is the indication that we are living the good life. When we exercise in moderation, we feel good about ourselves because we did just the right thing, in the right proportion, in the right way. The sweetness of the Golden Mean is that it gives us energy to exercise proper judgment about every important domain in our lives.

Without the restraint of the middle path, an idealist can easily become a self-defeating perfectionist. Overdoing takes the order out of your life. When we repeatedly overdo, we risk losing our way and even our life.

I don't want to do anything to let Aristotle down, but more important, I don't want to let myself down. I feel grateful to know that I have an inner compass that guides me. We should keep an even keel in order not to keel over. We want to be self-possessed, not possessed! The best things in life can be ruined if we overdo.

MODERATION IN ALL THINGS.

—*Terence*

10

Accept Impermanence
and Change

ONE *CAN* REMAIN ALIVE . . . IF ONE IS
UNAFRAID OF CHANGE, INSATIABLE IN
INTELLECTUAL CURIOSITY, INTERESTED IN
BIG THINGS, AND HAPPY IN SMALL WAYS.

—*Edith Wharton*

If you don't accept impermanence, you're going to be miserable. A huge part of our daily reality is that everything that lives will die. Nothing is everlasting in its current form. We're all transient visitors on our beloved planet earth. We're born, we experience illness, we grow old, and we die. Just as the planets orbit the sun in an orderly way, so our lives follow orderly patterns from conception to birth to death, and when we're fortunate, we're able to grow old gracefully with the time to contemplate our lives from the highest point of view. The foundation of life is this truth: everything in the universe is always changing. It is essential that we accept this first principle or we will always be suffering.

The Buddha became enlightened when he realized that suffering is part of the passage for every sentient being and unless we accept that absolutely everything will change, we will remain in the darkness of misery. When we experience a perfect moment, we know it won't last and understand it can never be repeated in the same way. And when awfulness comes, it, too, will not last. The death of a loved one, when we sit in sadness, feeling raw grief over an irreplaceable soul no longer living, moves from the present to the past. Time does heal. Grief does not last forever. When our dear friend and artist Roger Mühl suddenly died last April, the shock made me feel ill. I dreamed the first night after he died that it was just a nightmare. He was alive and thriving, coming to New York City for festivities in his honor, coming to Stonington to see our Atlantic coast that reminds us of his beloved Brittany, flying to Paris to help Peter and me celebrate our anniversary. I awoke and discovered he was in fact dead; my dream was just a dream.

We held a tribute for Roger in New York. We toasted him at the dinner that had been planned in his honor at La Grenouille, a mutually favorite French restaurant, where his spirit-energy was everywhere. The sadness of losing Roger, of never being able to see his smiling face again, became a happy celebration of this man who was bigger than life, who taught us how to see the wonder and majesty all around us in nature. We are all still living with Roger, but in a different way.

In my book *Happiness for Two*, the first essay is titled "Treat Each

Encounter as Though It Could Be Your Last." When we do so, every encounter is illumined. All the beauty and splendor, the happiness and joy are remembered, and we carry these with us as we move into the unknown. The present becomes the past and the past lives eternally in the present.

When we become comfortable with change as the universal principle of life, death becomes a natural part of living and makes us live each breath as our only time to live this very moment. To better accept our life cycles, we should pay more attention to the lessons of change that nature constantly sets before us: tides coming in and going out, the cycles of the moon, and the seasons of nature. Spring faithfully follows winter.

When we accept the laws of life—those things we cannot change, and the inevitable changes that are taking place inside and all around us—we can embrace making positive, appropriate changes in our lives. We can change our mind under changing circumstances; we can improve our environment through constructive changes that we choose. We can anticipate fresh beginnings, variety, and new interests as we develop our gifts. When we embrace the changes we have the power to implement, we rejuvenate ourselves. For forty-seven years I loved practicing interior design all over the world. In 2007, when Peter and I gave up our New York City residence, I closed my interior design office. I've changed and my career choice needed to change also in order to free my time to study my master teacher, Aristotle. Changing careers is stimulating and helps us to stay open and humble to learn more, to stretch ourselves, to tackle tough assignments.

The Roman poet Ovid understood that "all things change; nothing perishes." Things merely change their form. As Marcus Aurelius taught us, "Everything is in a state of metamorphosis." We're all in transformation: the caterpillar, the wormlike, hairy larva of a butterfly, develops into a monarch (or other) butterfly. Something that once crawled around the ground becomes something that metamorphosed into something that flies.

This same process happens to our children: they are utterly dependent on us in the beginning, and when they are adults, they love us and leave us. I'll never forget being in Avignon, France, with Peter, Alexandra, and Brooke, and at breakfast one morning our daughters announced they were going to ditch us and take an earlier train to Paris and would see us at dinner. They knew Paris well, spoke the language, and were old enough to shop and get around without being under the restrictive thumb of their parents. We suddenly realized our daughters were capable of spreading their own wings. This is change; this is as it should be.

ALL IS FLUX, NOTHING STAYS STILL . . .
THERE IS NOTHING PERMANENT EXCEPT CHANGE.

—Heraclitus

11

Be the Person You're Meant to Be

BUT BE NOT AFRAID OF GREATNESS.
SOME ARE BORN GREAT, SOME ACHIEVE
GREATNESS, AND SOME HAVE GREATNESS
THRUST UPON 'EM.

—Shakespeare

Who are the people you know and love who are bigger than life? These people are usually dedicated, disciplined, and of high energy and integrity. Aristotle teaches that we are all born in the dark cave of ignorance and evolve into greatness by steady effort. As Shakespeare notes, some are born great, but the seed needs to take root in order to blossom. Some people are afraid of their own greatness.

I believe everyone has a destiny and they have to hug it, care for it, and preserve it. Once you know what your destiny is, you have to follow it and use every muscle in your mind to nurture your potential greatness. No one else will ever fully understand us, but when you have the courage to nurture your seeds of greatness, life is transformed. Claude Monet, a giant among artists, said he was good for nothing but painting and gardening. He shaped and fashioned his whole life around his great gifts.

Some people have an epiphany when suddenly their destiny becomes clear, while others gradually evolve into their passion. On our last visit to see Roger Mühl, I asked him when he began to paint. His greatness appeared early: by age three he was drawing brilliantly, and by age seven he was doing portraits of everyone he knew. Giants such as he pursue their hero's journey daily; they hone themselves—mind, body, and soul—to explore their divine nature, daring to plumb the mysteries of the unknown.

Great people empower themselves in order to be the person they are meant to be. Some great souls are so far ahead of their time that they die before they are recognized. True artists and poets of life don't look outside for recognition but keep their inner flame burning brightly as they struggle to give birth to something new.

Great people have an inner enthusiasm that thrusts them into their research or canvas or paper. In my book *Things I Want My Daughters to Know,* I wrote to Alexandra and Brooke specifically: "Always remember your greatness." This goes for you, the mother, and you, the child. If a mother can instill this belief in her child, the child will be able to develop and unfold the great power within.

Aristotle warns that genius has a touch of madness. It is this fire that is so important, and although we as parents can't possibly be able to fully comprehend our children's unique potential, we must not stand in the way of their light.

Equally important, mothers must remember their responsibility to themselves. After the child leaves home and is on his own, Margaret Mead, the American anthropologist, urges women to enjoy postmenopausal zest and carry on in the exciting process of being the people they are meant to be.

Peter and I believe we were meant to be together. I know from our "happiness for two" that he is my other half, and it was providential that our paths crossed. I've interviewed dozens of women who feel that they were meant to be partners for life with their soul mate. If Peter hadn't dared to marry me, I can't imagine the opportunities we would have missed. Alexandra and Brooke would not have had Peter as a loving, kind, wise guide. We've loved each other for fifty-five years now, and have been married for thirty-five years. Only one person we knew believed in our union. John Bowen Coburn, my minister and friend, also a friend of Peter's, believed we were meant to be together. We were fortunate, because he married us! One person can make all the difference in our lives and encourage our journey toward our personal greatness.

The Buddhist monk, writer, translator, and photographer Matthieu Ricard prays, "May every moment of my life and the lives of others be one of wisdom, flourishing and inner peace." Flourishing. What a huge concept. When we flourish we grow luxuriantly, we thrive, we flower. In the words of the British poet John Keats, "Let us open our leaves like a flower." Together let us be the best people we are meant to be, right here, right now.

RESPONSIBILITY IS THE PRICE OF GREATNESS.

—Winston Churchill

12

Deal with Both Outer and Inner Circumstances

MAN IS NOT A CREATURE OF CIRCUMSTANCES.
CIRCUMSTANCES ARE CREATURES OF MEN.

—*Disraeli*

There are two kinds of circumstances: the constant swirl outside of us, and what is happening inside us. Happiness is not based on outer circumstances, often outside of our control; happiness is up to us and us alone. Whenever we find fault with conditions of our life beyond our control, we will suffer. The Buddha teaches, "Look within, thou art the Buddha." The stronger our mindfulness, the better we can deal with the outer circumstances of our lives.

Outside conditions depend on a wide range of factors and people, but what we think and how we act in all circumstances is up to us alone. Our inner life can't be delegated. Our integrity depends on our ability to maintain our inner soundness, regardless of what is going on around us.

One day a few months ago, I was peacefully beginning to write in my writing room at the cottage. Because there is no door between our adjoining writing rooms, Peter thoughtfully went downstairs to make a phone call in order not to disturb me. He fell on the bottom step. He asked me to feel his right kneecap. There was a huge indented area just above the knee. I called 911.

After spending the day in the emergency room, Peter was diagnosed as having a sprained knee and sent home with a prescription for painkillers. No walker, no crutches, no wheelchair. I knew he couldn't manage the steps to our house, so I called the Inn at Stonington and inquired if they had a room for us. Lesley, a friend, answered the telephone. She had heard from a mutual friend that Peter had an injury. Lesley had the good sense to beg a local nursing home to loan us a walker until we could buy one the next day. The inn is magnificent and our view of the water was healing, but Peter was not faring well. The medications he was given, taken on an empty stomach, made him feel awful. It also turned out that Peter had a complete rupture of his right quadricep tendon. He needed surgery. It's miraculous he didn't have another fall: there was nothing holding his knee together.

After several days at a rehabilitation facility following the surgery, we returned to the inn, but this time we asked for a handicapped-accessible room. We felt safe and this was an ideal place to recuperate.

When outer circumstances surprise us, our inner resources must guide us. Sometimes, our initial response is resistance. At first, we resisted hearing that Peter needed surgery. Obviously having been diagnosed with a sprained knee sounds better than needing surgery—but not if the knee wasn't sprained but all the tendons were ruptured! The surgeon rearranged his schedule and asked Peter to be at the hospital the next morning at 7:30 A.M. With reflection we saw that the sooner the operation was done, the sooner the healing could begin. This is what happens when we calmly manage our inner circumstances: resistance gives way to acceptance and then we can work on getting our life back to normal.

Peter got into a groove, using being laid up as a golden opportunity to study Buddhism. After all, he was seated for hours in a chair on a cushion—how convenient for learning to meditate and train his mind to be peaceful!

What are some challenges you're facing right now? How well equipped do you feel you are to accept your situation? The "ideal man," Aristotle teaches, "bears the accidents of life with dignity and grace, making the best of circumstances." Peter was Aristotelian in his grace and dignity. He never complained, never felt sorry for himself, and continuously counted his blessings—beginning with our dear friend, Bill Griffin, the innkeeper at the Inn at Stonington.

Bill called doctor friends to examine Peter and offer a second opinion. He arranged for a doctor to take us as patients now that we are Connecticut residents. He drove us to the doctor's offices and from the rehabilitation center to the inn. When Peter landed in the hospital in another ambulance the next morning, thanks to Bill a heart doctor was waiting in the emergency room. These and other blessed outer circumstances were life-giving and potentially life-saving. We accepted them with profound gratitude.

A doctor once wisely told me that we have to all work around the circumstances of our lives. We can't always choose what happens, but we can always be in charge of how we handle ourselves. The French philosopher and physician Albert Schweitzer knew that "harmony and strength exist in our lives only when our outer selves match our inner selves." We make the best of every circumstance when we are well and whole inside, alive to how fortunate we are.

CIRCUMSTANCES! I MAKE CIRCUMSTANCES.

—*Napoleon Bonaparte*

13

In Difficulty, Rethink Everything

HEARTS OPENED, MISFORTUNES
WERE PUT OUT OF MIND.

—*Nikos Kazantzakis*

Write down some of the difficult situations you are faced with right now. Perhaps you are in financial difficulty, or your spouse is going through some emotional problems, or your child is on drugs. Perhaps you're dealing with elderly parents who aren't able to make their own decisions. If your own life is without any serious present problems, think for a moment of the situations you've faced in the past and remember how you coped.

When you're facing difficulty, don't be afraid to rethink everything. Good mothers know that there are times to take big steps. Radical steps. We go on full alert and need to act with good judgment as we make painfully important, even life-or-death, decisions.

Don't be afraid of trusting your instincts. If your child's fever spikes in the middle of the night, go to the emergency room at a nearby hospital. Don't gloss over the truth, hoping your child will be better by morning. When Alexandra was four her fever went up to 108 degrees and ice packs and baby aspirin were not helping. Off we went to the hospital, where she was put on a freezing mattress to lower her fever and then in an oxygen tent. Don't mess around with issues of safety and health.

We only complicate a situation if we can't face it squarely. In interior design a rule that always works is: whenever you change one thing, rethink everything. In human life, one shift in reality affects everything else.

Sometimes we're so afraid of bad, sad news that we ignore difficulties, hoping they'll go away. A mother struggling to maintain everything at work and at home can put a difficulty out of her mind, not wanting to face it. One woman knew she needed new brakes in her car, but she kept putting it off because she didn't have a thousand dollars to pay for new ones. Her husband drove the car and asked her how long the brakes had been shot. "Three months." Her delay could have caused an accident, and she was driving her daughter around in her car during this time. She could have swallowed her pride in being financially self-sufficient and borrowed money from her husband, who had ample resources. We must admit when our rainy day comes and act responsibly.

Last year, when Peter fell in our cottage and tore his quadricep tendon, we had to quickly rethink our living situation. We chose to stay in the gracious charm of our favorite inn, where we could focus on his rehabilitation without the distractions of domestic life. Our motto was SAFETY, HAPPINESS, AND HEALTH. We realized that the bathrooms in our cottage were dangerous for anyone, especially the young and the old. Then we realized that if safety was our first priority, we needed to rethink our house. We entirely tore our cottage apart. When we bought and renovated a dilapidated eighteenth-century cottage in 1988, we intended to use it as a getaway. Now this is our home, and we needed to make it more suitable for year-round living.

Peter's physical therapist said that 80 percent of people who have knee surgery become depressed because they can't do everything for themselves. We consider ourselves so fortunate because we have each other. As we renovated our cottage to make it safe and sound, we realized how happy we were. The injury and surgery were a setback, but we understood it was only temporary. Thomas Merton reminds us, "When we are strong, we are always much greater than the things that happen to us."

Happiness is a key ingredient in healing. We were together in a loving environment with a beautiful view of the harbor. We loved watching the sunsets from the terrace, where we also enjoyed the gift of fresh air while our cottage was filled with sawdust and plaster dust. We were truly blessed, and when we have safety and happiness, health is encouraged. In our time of need, our daughter Brooke suggested we put in an outdoor shower in the Zen garden. The plumbing is right there in the kitchen. What a treat that has proven to be for us and for our grandchildren coming home after playing and swimming at the beach.

When we're forced to rethink everything, we have an opportunity to improve our safety, our happiness, and our health. Difficulty is important because without a cause, we don't have the effect: a golden opportunity to become wiser.

PATIENCE SAFEGUARDS OUR PEACE
OF MIND IN THE FACE OF ADVERSITY.

—*The Dalai Lama*

14

Simplify as You Go

IF WE DO MORE WITH LESS, OUR
RESOURCES WILL BE ADEQUATE TO
TAKE CARE OF EVERYBODY.

—Buckminster Fuller

Last year when we were having the cottage renovated we lived a quiet life in touch with nature. We got down to basics, living in one small room. By simplifying the details of our everyday living arrangements, we were able to spend our time reading, writing, and soon walking in the village we love.

The first few weeks were Zen simple. The room was clean, crisp, and attractively decorated in blue and white. There was a large chair where Peter liked to sit, a desk where I worked, the most comfortable bed ever, an end table, and a chest of drawers. Gradually I brought things from the cottage—stools, lamps, books, notebooks, and files. We always had fresh flowers on the window ledges. My desk area became too cluttered for writing. I set up my ironing board, adjusted it to desk height, and covered it with a white bath towel. Ahhh. Pure, clean, white space.

But over time, the ironing board became a catch-all for mail, bills, and letters. News of Peter's injury caused a flurry of gifts that got displayed around the room. The sink area became filled with toiletry items. The single closet got messy and stuffed.

Matthieu Ricard knew the secret to enlightenment: "Simplifying one's life to extract its quintessence is the most rewarding of all the pursuits." But most of us don't live in a monastery. We all have stuff that accumulates. There are many necessary details in our lives. How can we simplify as we go?

Peter and I realized that we had to take the advice of Marcus Aurelius and "get to the heart of the matter, to the essence of things." We were more disciplined about what we put on display. Newspapers and magazines were regularly recycled. We clipped out articles to save and filed them away. All reading and writing materials were stored in tote bags. We valued the Zen spa atmosphere of our room and worked daily to maintain its calmness and order. Because our space was small, we spent more time on a terrace overlooking the water. We learned not to complicate our lives by attempting to go home prematurely to a mess or bringing the "mess" to the inn. In the process, we learned how little it takes to be happy.

We can't enjoy inner peace if we scatter ourselves in every direction. Don't make life more difficult than it already is by neglecting to simplify as you go. I asked mothers how they managed. Here is some of their practical wisdom:

- *In good weather, keep your children out-of-doors as much as possible. This creates less wear and tear on the house and everyone is more relaxed.*
- *Buy in bulk and shop with a list of essentials. Don't wander the aisles, or you'll be tempted to buy things you don't need.*
- *Refuse to waste your time buying something and then returning it. Your resolve will force you to make intelligent purchases you can put to immediate use.*
- *At the grocery checkout, bag freezer items, refrigerator items, and bathroom toiletries separately.*
- *Set the breakfast table the night before in order to free up your morning.*
- *As soon as the mail arrives, recycle all unwanted items, sort bills from letters, and try to pay the bills immediately so that they don't weigh on your mind.*
- *Buy pre-roasted chicken at the grocery store.*
- *Keep a stroller in the car trunk stocked with extra wipes.*
- *Every two or three months, "weed out" the children's toys and donate them.*
- *Lay out the children's clothes the night before.*
- *Lay out your clothes the night before.*
- *Write reminders on sticky notes and put them where you will see them—on the bathroom mirror or the refrigerator door.*

- *Regularly put your rooms on a diet. Remove extraneous items and stacks of papers.*
- *Have one place for wallet or bag, keys, sunglasses, and pens. Misplacing necessary items causes chaos.*
- *In a shady area, instead of maintaining grass, use a hardy ground cover. Garden in pots for easy weeding, watering, and portability.*
- *Instead of joining a gym, save money and time by playing in the yard or on the playground with your children or grandchildren.*
- *As appropriate, bring your children with you wherever you go. They don't care where they go as much as they care to be with you.*
- *On errands or trips, travel with everything you might need in order not to waste money, time, and gas buying drinks, snacks, or forgotten necessities.*
- *Have a picnic bag ready with all the necessary containers in order to easily add food and be ready to go.*
- *Color-coordinate your and the children's travel clothes so that all items mix and match.*
- *When traveling, use Ziploc bags to store small items—crayons, beads, cards, and puzzle pieces. When packing suitcases, use large plastic bags to keep clothes in categories and to prevent wrinkling.*
- *Take a relaxing and inexpensive vacation at home and spend time as a family doing craft projects, writing stories, drawing, reading, and going on outings that are mutually enjoyable.*

Even notoriously complex and costly things such as renovations can be subjected to the "simplify as you go" approach. When we renovated our bathrooms in the cottage I requested the simplest solutions to achieve our goal of safety. No extra flourishes or embellishments. When we "do more with less," we feel better about ourselves because we are helping our planet home.

My favorite artist and friend Roger Mühl taught me the beauty of simplifying. One memorable lunch on their terrace in Mougins, France, consisted of hardboiled eggs split in two with a dollop of mayonnaise on top, a bowl of baby lettuces from their garden drizzled with oil and mustard dressing, a plate of cheese and sweet pears.

Let us be content with less and, like Matthieu Ricard, consider our possessions as tools. There is great beauty in keeping things simple in order to be able to joyfully appreciate our family and friends in relaxed, cheerful ways. Let's all strive to become kitchen-table simple; this is at the heart and soul of an authentic life well lived.

WE DO NOT LIVE MORE FULLY MERELY BY
DOING MORE, SEEING MORE, TASTING
MORE, AND EXPERIENCING MORE.

—*Thomas Merton*

15

Grandmothers: The Wisdom of Experience

BECOMING A GRANDPARENT IS A SECOND CHANCE.
FOR YOU HAVE ONE CHANCE TO PUT TO USE ALL THE
THINGS YOU LEARNED THE FIRST TIME AROUND AND
MAY HAVE MADE MISTAKES ON. IT'S ALL LOVE AND
NO DISCIPLINE. THERE'S NO THORN IN THIS ROSE.

—Dr. Joyce Brothers

Now that I am a grandmother, I feel the joy of being a special treat for our grandchildren, who are simply the bright light of our lives. I'm looking forward to taking them on trips and being an Auntie Mame to them, much as my Aunt Betty was to me when she took me on a trip around the world. The mutual influence between grandchild and grandparent is a wise and wonderful one. The relationship is one of celebration, full of laughter, play, fun, and games.

Good mothers let grandmothers do their thing. Everyone benefits from tapping into the wisdom of the generations. Children need adoring older people in their lives. Grandparents need the energy and innocence children bring. Daniel Gilbert, the author of the best-selling book *Stumbling on Happiness*, knows what makes him happy: "You couldn't pay me $100,000 to miss a play date with my granddaughters," he said in an interview in the *New York Times*, "and that is not because I'm rich. That's because I know that a hundred grand won't make me as happy as nurturing my relationship with my granddaughters will."

With luck, grandparents see the splendid job their children are doing raising the next generation, and everyone relaxes into the delicious experience. We don't all have these perfect relationships, but we can make even less-than-wonderful ties work when motivated by the benefits to the children. A great aunt can be adorable in her devotion.

Having an elderly person who lives nearby may also be a blessing. I had dear, sweet Mrs. Walton who, it turned out, owned the field where I picked daffodils and, along with my five- and six-year-old friends, sold them back to her for our junior garden club project. She served us birch beer and gingersnaps at her kitchen table, was interested in hearing all our stories, and made us feel as though we were the most important people on earth. Older people have a deliberate, slower-moving style that makes young people feel heard and safe.

Grandmothers are allowed to abandon cooking, ironing, and doing laundry in favor of spending time amusing the "grands." Be it craft projects, storytelling, reading or writing, showing off skills on the bike, or playing ball, no one is cuter, smarter, sweeter, more coordinated or perfect than our grandchildren.

Grandchildren intuitively show off for us and are on their *best, best* behavior. Grandparents know never to discipline their grands because that task is so beautifully handled by their parents. While we enjoy the results of their discipline, at the same time I choose not to undermine or interfere.

Good mothers know the value of grandparents' generational wisdom. We tell wildly funny stories of what their mother was like when she was a little girl, and when we reinforce the stories with pictures, we have endless laughs.

Here are ten things grandmothers know:

1) We're never in a rush, never too busy for time with the grandchildren.

2) We have two free hands to hug them, hold them, and help them at work or play.

3) In their eyes, we don't have anything to do but have fun with them.

4) We often let them win at games. We know they love to feel we're a little old and not as "with it" as they are.

5) We always have some of their favorite treats on hand, not just on "special" occasions.

6) We tell outrageous stories about when we were little. "You didn't have TV, Grandma?" "You didn't have computers, Grandma?" Great giggles.

7) We always come bearing gifts. Even the most modest

presents are wrapped with fun paper and lots of pretty ribbon with fun cards saying loving things.

8) We are excellent listeners. We ask the names of stuffed animals and dolls, and inquire about friends, teachers, and what our grandchildren love most about school.

9) We treasure every note, drawing, and painting, and have our grandchild's artwork featured in our home. We carry a "brag" book of photographs.

10) When a grandchild invites his grandmother to come play, she's *there*, and whatever game or adventure she experiences is the thrill of her lifetime. She never had this much fun when she was young!

Grandmothers let grandchildren know that they are the most important people in her life. When children feel this intimate, caring bond, this supportive environment creates a secure feeling that extends throughout their lifetime. In her classic book *Gift from the Sea*, Anne Morrow Lindbergh reflected on her grandmother's influence: "So many things we love are you, I can't seem to explain except by little things, by flowers and beautiful hand-made things—small stitches. So much of our . . . thinking—so many sweet customs . . . It is all *you*. I hadn't realized it before. This is so vague, but do you see a little, dear Grandma? I want to thank you."

Grandmothers, too, blossom with their accumulated knowledge and experience. Madeleine L'Engle wrote of her grandmother: "She seems to have had the ability to stand firmly on the rock of her past while living completely and unregretfully in the present."

This is the greatest treasure—to be part of the life of our children's children. How can we ever show enough appreciation to our children for creating all this joy?

THE CLOSEST FRIENDS I HAVE MADE ALL THROUGH LIFE HAVE BEEN PEOPLE WHO ALSO GREW UP CLOSE TO A LOVED AND LOVING GRANDMOTHER OR GRANDFATHER.

—Margaret Mead

16

Make Wise Emotional Attachments

THE GOOD THINGS OF LIFE ARE NOT TO BE HAD
SINGLY, BUT COME TO US WITH A MIXTURE.

—Charles Lamb

One day last spring, a blue hydrangea plant in my hand, I was headed to the cottage to greet guests attending my writer's retreat when the telephone rang and I learned the shocking news that our dear friend, the artist Roger Mühl, had died in his sleep just hours before. I went from being sublimely happy and anticipating the day to feeling heavier than lead. I cried out in agony. I walked like a zombie, in fear of falling. I wasn't ready to accept this bad news. Death is so final. I could not absorb the reality of it.

I told my guests the sad news, and I read the first essay from *Happiness for Two*: "Treat Each Encounter as Though It Were Your Last." Crying, I pointed to the paintings around us: sun-washed rooftops, blue skies of the South of France, profusions of flowers—all the work of my dear friend.

I will never forget the tenderness and compassion of my seminar guests. Before we began the writer's conference that afternoon, we unanimously voted to have lunch on the water at Skipper's Dock. We all had a sip or two of a favorite Pinot Gris from Oregon. What seemed to be the darkest day evolved into a poignant celebration of a genius artist who transformed my life. Roger was my muse. He taught me to always live my passion. In a friendship that lasted almost half a century, I have been inspired by his art and his vision of how to live the good life every day.

Roger's death made me aware of the stages of healing and letting go. I wanted more of his life-sustaining energy, his flashing smile, his laughter, and his unflinching belief in beauty. I wanted him to continue to paint his colorful, sun-drenched canvases. We had plans to attend his upcoming show in New York City. We were going to invite him to stay at the inn in Stonington Village. We'd planned to visit him at his home in Mougins. I'd hoped our grandchildren could enjoy his amazing spirit. Of all the friendships I've ever had, ours was the most pure, the most mutually understanding. He never, for a moment, caused me an ounce of pain.

The British writer C. S. Lewis reminds us, "Bereavement is a universal and integral part of our experience of love." I was definitely suffering the loss of a loved one, and I will never "get over" Roger Mühl. But slowly, my sadness turned to awe and appreciation for this life-changing friendship. I am no longer clinging to what might have been if he were still living.

Loss can turn to gratitude. Only something profound can cause such grief. The great lesson love teaches us is to appreciate deeply right here, right now, what we have. I do try to treat each encounter as though it could be the last, and I try not to assume anything about the future. Many mothers told me they wish they could "bottle" their child and keep the clock from ticking. Yet certain losses come with the territory. Mothers worry, walk the floor, and think sometimes they can't stand the pain of loving and letting go. All normal children will leave their parents if they are able. Some leave earlier than others. I left home at sixteen to travel and live in New York City with my aunt. I realized years later that my mother was jealous of Aunt Betty for her ability, unfettered by the responsibilities of marriage and motherhood, to take her three oldest nieces around the world.

The enlightened mother acknowledges that her child is not an extension of her, not an object to possess. We are temporary custodians of our child's soul. Things may happen we can't foresee or control. We must remember that our caring and loving evolve in unity with our children's evolution from dependence to independence, and that this powerful drive for maturity is their birthright. We are here to nourish our children's soul as it passes through our sphere of influence. Our job is to let children grow up and spread their wings. We risk that they might not love us or respect our values. Even if they adore us, they may cancel our vote in a presidential race and develop different spiritual beliefs. They rarely leave the nest neat and tidy.

Good mothers keep their core identity and let children have theirs.

This is fundamental to wise emotional attachment. We should practice wise attachment with our children every day, encouraging them to become increasingly independent, self-confident, flourishing beings. Gradually we separate ourselves from the intimacy of their daily lives. It can be painfully difficult to disconnect, but this is our responsibility and duty as parents.

There will be a failed math test or two, but whether the grades are good or bad, they are not our grades. When a child makes mistakes, good mothers do not take it personally. Somehow children grow up and in most cases turn out all right, in spite of us! They are children of the universe, and we have the privilege of caring for them in their formative years. The more loving we are, the less possessive and demanding we become.

True love is selfless love. When we have unhealthy attachments to our children, we force them to be loyal to us rather than to their natural inclination to love us in return for our healthy selflessness. We should focus on how grateful we are to have been blessed with the enormous opportunity to nurture this sacred human being, and gladly let go.

When we are successful in this essential parent-child process, everyone benefits. We can feel great joy in our child's accomplishments and especially in their happiness. They can honor us, yet thrive apart from us. Mindfully love selflessly, and know that there is no better way to live and love than to be emotionally wise in our attachments.

WE NEVER ATTACH OURSELVES LASTINGLY
TO ANYTHING THAT HAS NOT COST
US CARE, LABOR AND LONGING.

—*Balzac*

17

Don't Look Back

THE SECRET OF HEALTH FOR BOTH THE MIND AND BODY
IS NOT TO MOURN FOR THE PAST, NOT TO WORRY ABOUT
THE FUTURE, NOR TO ANTICIPATE TROUBLES, BUT TO LIVE
THE PRESENT MOMENT WISELY AND EARNESTLY.

—*The Buddha*

The past has no life force. It is over. What you can do about current situations is what is in your hands. Whether you reminisce about the good old days or regret all the things that went wrong, the past is the only part of your life you can't improve or change. Nostalgia doesn't make us as happy as we might think. When we dwell on the past, it is hard for us to get our life force in high gear. I read about a poet in the *New York Times* several years ago. One of his poems ended, "bury it without a funeral." Hear, hear.

In 1959 Peter bought a large apartment in New York City—with Peter, his wife, and six children, this family needed space. When Peter and I married in 1974, I moved to Peter's apartment with my two daughters, ages six and four. The family-oriented neighborhood was ideal with its schools, churches, museums, and parks. By 2007, we had lived our life chapter there fully, and it was time for Peter and me to move on.

Once we made up our minds, we only looked forward. When we walked out of our apartment building for the last time, the doorman inquired, "When are you moving out, Mr. Brown?" Peter smiled. "Right now." We'd agreed to walk south to the street corner and keep walking. We never looked back. Now, when we visit New York, we stay in a hotel in an entirely different neighborhood. We love being tourists in our former home base, going to museums and fully appreciating a city we love. Friends ask if we miss it. I feel a weight has been lifted. I adore being on vacation in New York City.

We all owe a great deal of gratitude for the experiences that brought us where we are today. But we must all move onward and upward with the least amount of extraneous baggage possible.

My spiritual mentor John Bowen Coburn believes that we live life in chapters. The more fully we embrace each, the more free we are to open a new, exciting chapter in our journey of discovery. Emerson teaches us, "The world is new, untried: Do not believe in the past. I give you the universe a virgin today." He believed that every ending is a beginning. Think of an ending that is happening in your life. What is the beginning hidden within it? When we embrace the future without dragging the past with us, we look at what's before us with a fresh heart.

We will never wake up in the morning and greet *tomorrow*. We always greet *today*, the new, present day. We open our eyes, and we are in this present. There is no way we can predict what will happen even in the next second. The lessons of the past can help us avoid some difficulties, but we can only learn the lessons of the present by living it now.

Consider who you can be today, not who you were yesterday. Good mothers know not to label their children. They know no one should be defined by who they once were. For example, I am no longer interested in doing interior design; I'd rather study Aristotle, write and speak about life and living, or have a play date with a grandchild. Most important, I want to spend my days and nights with Peter.

Good mothers don't look back. A shy child at four blossoms at age thirteen in an accepting, loving environment. As my friend Toni understands, "Your now does not have to be forever." If we don't label a child as being shy, we free her spirit to evolve. We are all evolving. We should treat each person as they are in the present moment, not as they were in the past. Our personal development depends on moving beyond the limits of the past to embrace the new day, the new breath we take, our opportunity to make a meaningful contribution now, right where we are.

Gently close the door of the past and face the open door before you. What you have accomplished pales in comparison with what you can do with your talents right now. Use your accumulated knowledge and wisdom to take the leap of faith and do something gutsy, bold, and noble. You are equipped for whatever you are passionate about accomplishing. Make your mark on earth's five billion years. Now is your only chance. Emerson counsels us: "Finish every day and be done with it. You have done what you could; some blunders and absurdities have crept in; forget them as soon as you can. Tomorrow is a new day; you shall begin it serenely and with too high a spirit to be encumbered with old non-sense."

The saddest words in any language are "what might have been." Aristotle knew even the gods can't change the past. The future has arrived. The hour has come. Embrace all the possibilities today offers. Reach high and trust your brilliance. Everything you have ever thought or done has been necessary preparation for this moment.

I TELL YOU THE PAST IS A BUCKET OF ASHES.

—*Carl Sandburg*

18

Make Space to Breathe

To attain knowledge, add things
every day. To attain wisdom,
remove things every day.

—Tao Te Ching

When I first visited Japan in 1959, I became fascinated by the brilliant concept of "space to breathe." Every house was spare, clean, lean with empty spaces. Behind fabric-covered sliding screens, beautiful objects were neatly placed on shelves. Few were in view because too many objects seen at once would cause visual confusion. I never slept better than on the futon placed on the straw tatami matting used as floor covering in Japanese houses and inns. What a revelation: no need for a bed! This experience fifty years ago has shaped my awareness ever since. Since grasping the virtue of "space to breathe," I've tried to live by Lao-Tzu's wise advice: "empty and be full."

Good mothers need their inner space. This space to breathe is always available to us, ever present, here, now, in our breath—but how often we snuff out this calm, expansive peace of mind because of the demands of daily life, feeling too busy to find and rest in this essential inner space.

None of us can afford to ignore our need to build an inner world where we can achieve peace of mind. By regularly turning inward to this vast space, we can unfetter our lives, tap our deepest ability to cope, train our mind to think positively, and achieve lasting happiness.

We now know through scientific research that we can change our brain chemistry by calmly making space to breathe. The chemical neurologist, researcher, and Zen practitioner Dr. James H. Austin examines the changes that occur in the brain as the result of long-term meditation. His books *Zen and the Brain* and *Zen-Brain Reflections* explore the connection between meditation and enlightened states.

Peace of mind is not the absence of problems, but rather the overcoming of suffering by training our mind to cope better. Inner space is where we turn to develop peace of mind.

His Holiness the Dalai Lama warns us not to confuse peace of mind with spaced-out insensitivity: "A true peaceful mind is very sensitive, very aware." When we explore our inner emptiness we're refreshed, able to accept new thoughts and embrace ideas in the expansiveness of solitude, quiet, and truth. We learn to be comfortable in this mindfulness.

When our life is overcrowded by people and tasks and we neglect the most important aspects of who we are, we risk burning out. We yearn to escape the world. But daily practice of meditation, prayer, study, and yoga enlarges the soul. Our inner space is a village, a lake, mountains, gardens, the expanse of the sky, the depth of the ocean. Our sense of separateness disappears. The only place to look for tranquility is in this sacred space.

Where do you go to make space to breathe? In *The Circle of Quiet*, Madeline L'Engle describes how she would disappear every afternoon to walk to a pond, dangle her legs, and make space for her inner world to awaken. I know someone who goes out in her rowboat. On the water, she listens to the silences.

"Meditation," wrote the Vietnamese Buddhist monk Thich Nhat Hanh, "is to be aware of what is going on—in our bodies, our feelings, our minds and the world. Life is both dreadful and wonderful. To practice meditation is to be in touch with both aspects. Don't think you have to be solemn to meditate. To meditate well, you have to smile a lot." It is the sense of immense spaciousness that brings us this joy. Here grace is found and we mysteriously become full—of light, love, kindness, and confidence that all is right with the world. Even when we doubt the oneness and wellness of the world, we can still experience the growing integration within.

I believe Emerson was right when he wrote that nothing can bring us peace but ourselves. Finding peace requires facing and accepting the elements that pull us in opposite directions. One of Peter's and my spiritual teachers, Dr. Eric Butterworth of Unity Church, taught us: "More important than learning how to recall things is finding ways to forget things that clutter the mind." The best way to live the good life is to seek harmony through a daily commitment to some form of inner exploration. As you breathe in new life and exhale, consciously appreciate the gift of your inner resources, the invisible wealth you possess in the limitless reservoir of your mysterious soul. The wise Roman emperor Marcus Aurelius knew that "nowhere can man find a quieter or more untroubled retreat than in his own soul."

Whether you go on a mindful walk alone, pause for a few seconds to marvel and give thanks when you contemplate the petals of a rose or the innocent face of a child, you can make space to breathe new life, great love, and abiding happiness. The more each of us makes space to breathe more deeply and more intentionally, the more peace will be on earth. One breath at a time, we can make a difference.

TAKE TIME TO LISTEN TO WHAT IS SAID
WITHOUT WORDS, TO OBEY THE LAW TOO SUBTLE
TO BE WRITTEN, TO WORSHIP THE UNNAMABLE
AND TO EMBRACE THE UNFORMED.

—*Lao-Tzu*

19

Know the Difference Between Needs and Wants

HAVING THE FEWEST WANTS,
I AM NEAREST TO THE GODS.

—*Socrates*

All of us should think about our lives with brutal honesty in order to separate our basic needs from our wants, our desires. Many lost souls are the ones who want this and want that, feeling continually unfulfilled. Incessant wants and endless desires drive people to their graves. When we're happy, we're satisfied with our life and tend to look at life from a grateful perspective.

Because we are surrounded by others purchasing the newest electronic gadget, the latest model car, or a large flat-screen television, if we aren't thinking clearly, we begin to brainwash ourselves, blurring the lines between what is essential to our well-being—what we really need—and what we'd ideally like to have. When we narrow things down to our fundamental needs and redirect our inner and outer resources toward worthwhile pursuits, we reduce much of the complexity of day-to-day living and increase our satisfaction. The nineteenth-century British historian and essayist Thomas Carlyle believed that "not what I have but what I do is my kingdom." Knowing what you don't need is a key to wisdom.

Daniel Kahneman, a Princeton psychologist who shared the 2002 Nobel Prize in economics, has written about the "aspiration treadmill." He says that we quickly adapt to an increase in income and within a few months aspire to something more. Bombarded with advertisements that make us feel needy, we yearn to acquire more things. Once we get stuck on the "aspiration treadmill," it's hard to jump off. The Greek philosopher Epicurus understood that "Whoever does not regard what he has as most ample wealth, is unhappy though he be master of the world."

How acquisitive do you rate yourself on a scale from 1 to 10? Do you feel you know the difference between your needs and your wants? Do you ever think your needs are so great that you can never be satisfied? Do you feel you have enough? Are there certain times in the past when you've been needy? Have you ever been greedy?

When we narrow things down to essentials, we discover what we most value. When I recently asked Peter what he needs, he said, "peace of mind." What do you most value? How can you bring it into your life? Are there some things you can get rid of that you thought you needed? Our needs and wants, as well as those of our children, are always evolving.

I've made a list of my basic needs for my chosen lifestyle, as well as a list of my wants. I feel extremely grateful that I can honestly say I don't need anything I don't already have, and if things change in the future, I have confidence I will have the necessary resources to meet my needs, judging from my experience in the past. I feel I have more than enough objects. I desire to live a leaner, cleaner, less cluttered life.

My Needs List (in no particular order)

- *To love and be loved*
- *Feel peace of mind*
- *Feel loving-kindness*
- *Food*
- *Shelter*
- *Quiet time to study, contemplate, and write*
- *Sufficient money to travel and be independent*
- *Flowers*
- *Books*
- *Paper*
- *Fountain pens*
- *Ink*
- *Eyeglasses*
- *Happiness*

My Wants List (in no particular order)

- *Travel*
- *Spend time with the grandchildren and children*
- *Write and publish books*
- *Spend time with Peter*
- *Give lectures*
- *Go to the hair salon*
- *Visit with friends*
- *Enjoy good wine with friends and loved ones*
- *Go to various restaurants*
- *Have a view of the ocean*
- *Have opportunities to exercise*
- *Have simple jewelry*
- *Buy clothes made in Hong Kong by Shanghai Tang*
- *Read newspapers*
- *Read our journalist daughter A. B. Stoddard's political articles*
- *Surround myself with people I trust who have good judgment*
- *Enjoy good health*
- *Embrace sunshine*
- *Experience the Atlantic sea air*
- *Have black truffles on special occasions*

What is on your lists? Review and revise your list every so often, because your needs and wants will change over time. We think we need certain things, but then realize they are wants. We may even realize we don't want some of the things we thought we needed! When Peter and I gave up our New York City apartment and sold or gave away many of its contents, we felt great relief. It was time to move on and let go.

Don't feel guilty about acknowledging your basic needs. When I interviewed Amanda, she told me with great certainty that surfing was a need. "This is for my mental health. I wish everyone could surf, to experience being one with the energy of the ocean." Another woman says her horse is definitely a need: "When the children were growing up, this was something I did for me versus being their mom. I love my children, and I love and need my horse."

If you determine you need more money, for example, set specific goals and calculate how much is enough. In order to have a better-paying job, what will you have to sacrifice? What will you do with the money? Perhaps you want your child to have ballet lessons. Try a few lessons and see if your child shows interest. If you want your child to learn how to swim, investigate lessons at a local Y.

Will your needs strain your time or financial resources? Will you need other people to help you? Emerson wisely mused, "Can anything be so elegant as to have few wants, and to serve them one's self?" Making your list will make you more aware of your life decisions. Ask yourself, "Is this necessary?" Oscar Wilde advises us to think twice: "In this world there are only two tragedies. One is not getting what one wants, and the other is getting it."

Rinzai, a Zen master, inquired of his students, "What, at this moment, is lacking?" When we live intensely in the vast spaciousness of the present, what we want may be exactly what we have—inner peace and satisfaction with life just as it is.

LET NOT YOUR MIND RUN ON WHAT YOU
LACK AS MUCH AS ON WHAT YOU HAVE ALREADY.
OF THE THINGS YOU HAVE, SELECT THE BEST; AND
THEN REFLECT HOW EAGERLY THEY WOULD
BE SOUGHT IF YOU DID NOT HAVE THEM.

—*Marcus Aurelius*

20

Write It Down

Last spring I led my first Writer's Happiness Retreat. All of the participants brought writing paraphernalia, leaving technology at home. To get us all in the flow, I suggested that everyone write the first two or three sentences of a letter to someone they dearly love. What fascinated me was the spontaneity and pleasure everyone took in putting words on paper.

In my interviews I learned how mothers, in coaching us through writing our thank-you letters, taught us about gratitude. This habit, ingrained in me from age four, has worked deeply into the fiber of my soul. To this day I can't truly appreciate the full richness of someone's generosity unless I write a note of thanks. It literally makes me feel good to write a thank-you note, and it is a gift I give myself.

Some of the best, most poignant writing is not in books or articles, but in everyday correspondence, letters exchanged, notes dashed off and sent, valentines lovingly posted, sweet thoughts on birthdays and graduations.

Most of us write more than we realize. Make a list of all the different ways you "write it down":

- *Grocery list*
- *"To do" list*
- *Diary or journal*
- *Scrapbook captions*
- *A toast for a wedding or a special event*
- *A speech or a presentation*
- *Travel diary*
- *Letter to a lover*
- *Letter to a child*
- *Thank-you letter*
- *Letters to honor the life of a dear friend or loved one who has died*
- *A poem*
- *A business report*
- *A legal document*
- *A contract*
- *A recipe*
- *An article*
- *A baby book*

As you can see, people who say they "can't write" actually write all the time. We remember things twice as well when we write them down, from the need to buy eggs to the date when our baby took her first steps. Whether we keep a record of the joy and the good times or reach out to others in their hour of sorrow or need, whenever we make the effort to write, we will feel enriched.

It's easy to get caught up in the flow of life and neglect to honor special moments. When our daughters were little, I carried pocket-size notebooks wherever we went in order to record their first words or their remarks and questions. What fun to pass this on to a child for a teenage birthday! When you leave a paper trail for your children and grandchildren, you are providing lasting memories, information, and inspiration. You'll never know how much your honest, loving words could mean to others.

Good mothers know the priceless value of writing a child a love letter. No matter what we say in conversation, when something is written down it becomes more permanent, a document that can be savored, saved, and treasured. E. B. White, a brilliantly insightful writer and teacher, observed, "Don't write about Man, write about a man."

At our Writer's Happiness Retreat I asked everyone to write the beginning of a letter to someone they love, to write their own obituary, and to write a eulogy to be given at their funeral (one they'd like for someone to say in tribute and praise).

William Faulkner said, "I never know what I think about something until I read what I've written." We discover ourselves in our writing, and our writing may help others to know themselves better. As soon as you have an important thought, write it down, even in cryptic form, in order not to lose it. No matter how busy your life is, try to express your love of life and your family in some form each day. Even if it is just a sticky note on the bathroom mirror to your spouse, a note inside a child's lunch box, or a postcard to a child in college, *write it down* today, and every day.

I'VE ALWAYS THOUGHT BEST WHEN I WROTE.
WRITING IS WHAT CENTERED ME. IN THE ACT OF
WRITING, I FELT MOST ALIVE, MOST COHERENT,
MOST STABLE AND MOST VULNERABLE.

—*Toni Morrison*

21

Clear the Clutter

A MAJOR CLEAR-OUT IS ESSENTIAL
IF YOU TRULY WANT TO HAVE PASSION,
JOY, AND HAPPINESS IN YOUR LIFE.

—Karen Kingston

A few years ago I was enjoying a wonderfully fun lunch party with several friends in a favorite Italian restaurant. Soon after the party began, we all started talking about "clutter clearing," a term I share with many of my friends, especially those who have young children. It seems something happens to all of us around mid-January: we have to get rid of the old to make way for the new.

With our New Year's resolutions freshly in place, we see the baggage we carry from the past. If only we can clear all the clutter from our lives, we'll be able to think clearly, act intelligently, and move ahead with energy and enthusiasm.

Mess slows us down. When we're not alert to the energy drain of clutter, we become emotionally and intellectually bogged down.

One of the books I'm most proud to have written is *Living a Beautiful Life: 500 Ways to Add Elegance, Order, Beauty, and Joy to Every Day of Your Life*. I've always believed that order promotes prosperity: when freedom from disorder is maintained, fresh, new, imaginative ideas can flower. Our goals become clearer, our heart expands to greater awareness of what's best for us and how we can proceed. Simply making an effort to live an orderly life fosters an aura of peace.

I want to get on with my life. I often want to make radical changes in order to clear away the past with a clean sweep and make way for the new, the unknown, the possibilities I long to explore.

As an interior design student I was instructed by Van Day Truex, a teacher I greatly admired who was president of Parsons School of Design in Paris and who later became the creative head of Tiffany & Co. His motto was, "Control, edit and distill."

One of my favorite lectures to give is titled Stress Reduction Through Aesthetics. Whenever my life is out of control, it always is visible in my surroundings. There's clutter everywhere—in my huge pocketbook stuffed with everything but the kitchen sink, on the crowded bathroom counters and end tables, in the stacks of papers on counters that should be used for meal preparation. I know I'm really in trouble when my writing table is junked up. Who has the energy to face all that negative energy, the confusion, the undecided, unfiled, neglected stuff?

Recently I was visiting with a friend and neighbor who spent the better part of a weekend clutter clearing. Tanja looked sparkling and crisp as she described to me her joy, and how much better she felt to have attacked the enemy. She likes waking up every morning to pure space and order.

Wanting to pass things on to loved ones, originally Tanja sorted through her overcrowded closet and drawers, making piles of items for her sister, her mother, and her niece. Each chair in her living room was piled high with the objects she was discarding, and, in her heart, couldn't wait to get rid of. Eventually she realized that no one in her family needed her cast-offs, and maybe they didn't even want them. In the end, she gathered it all into one big bundle for the thrift store.

Our New York apartment was so full of our combined family paraphernalia, our joint library books, my not-so-skimpy wardrobe of colorful clothes, my need for a "room-of-my-own," plus my interior design office/studio. As an interior designer I was a serious collector of beautiful objects as well as a hoarder of things I felt would enhance my work.

The paperwork involved in writing books, traveling, and giving talks kept adding to the clutter. Every time I was published in a magazine, I received dozens of tearsheets. Years passed. More upon more accumulated. Peter moved from a formal office to the apartment to do his legal and charity work. Things, quite frankly, were getting out of control. One day I was on the telephone with one of our daughters and she said with a laugh, "Mommy, I hope you don't expect us to know about your secret storage bin in the basement when you die."

No one wants to inherit someone else's mess. Once Peter and I decided to let go of the apartment, we realized we had our hands full. I had to be ruthless with the amazing amount of things we had stored, stuffed, shoved, squeezed, and forced into closets, drawers, under tables, into cabinets, and on countertops. Certain things became apparent:

- *I was alone with this task.*
- *No one wanted to help me.*
- *No one could help me!*
- *No one wanted to hear my complaints.*

Peter had to sort through all his legal files. This was a solitary sentimental journey he had to face alone. I, at the same time, had decided to give up my interior design business—along with almost fifty years of files, as well as my mother's design papers.

Then there were the books. Having raised eight children in this apartment, we were awash in schoolbooks, yearbooks, diaries, notebooks, and scrapbooks.

The apartment sold quickly, and we were grateful. But now the pressure was on to sort through this mountain of stuff. I had no time to be sentimental, but, at first, I tried. Everything I touched had been, at some point, extremely important to us. Some things still were, and it wasn't easy to part with them. My former boss and friend Eleanor McMillen Brown taught her designers, "Be careful what you throw out. You never know when something will be useful for a future project." But as I threw out hundreds of files and whole folders full of old information, records, and publicity, I began getting in the swing of getting rid of the old, making way for the new.

I grew to be lovingly ruthless in my quest to empty the apartment on time. I came to realize that I had to let go of approximately 95 percent of my files. I threw away almost every article that had been written about me, all the tapes of television appearances, most letters, children's old report cards and kindergarten artwork.

There were a few precious things I wanted to treasure, and they were saved. After deciding what to do with every object in the apartment, we came at last to Peter's collection of his fifty years of legal work: 303 volumes bound in blue and stamped in gold. These contained one lawyer's life's work—half a century's cases. The clock was ticking. We were literally down to the wire. Several attempts to place this pricelessly valuable collection of books failed. Family members, overwhelmed with clutter, didn't have the space. With everything else in the apartment moved out—to children, to thrift stores, or to storage—these books were the last remaining objects.

Over lunch one memorably soulful day, I tried to prepare Peter for the possibility that the last resort might be black lawn bags we'd have to put out onto the street.

Aristotle believed we all need good luck in order to thrive. Fortunately, luck was ours. Yale University, where Peter went to college and law school, sent two scholars from the library to examine the volumes. We'd always hoped Peter's legal cases would be placed where students and teachers could have them available in one collection for study and research. The Peter Megargee Brown papers were accepted by the Yale University library for its manuscript and archives department.

As we sort through all our stuff, we find the items that truly elevate us now. I have an ongoing determination to continuously be mindful about what I give "house room" to in order to clear the path for us to move toward greater inward clarity.

What do you want to give "house room" to? To get yourself started, pretend you have the pressure of a deadline. We've all noticed how tidy the house becomes when company is expected: a friend of mine spent two weeks clearing the clutter from her kitchen counters before her daughter and grandson arrived for a visit. Begin each day setting a kitchen timer for twenty minutes and attacking one pile, one box, one closet, or one drawer at a time. It is too intimidating to look at the whole picture without breaking it up into manageable sections. Make notes about your goals and feel the satisfaction of crossing things off one by one. Rather than stashing things away in temporary locations, figure out good places to put things you wish to save and store.

Looking back, I believe we made some really tough decisions, but I also believe we can trust our instincts to make wise choices. I've often said, when it comes to deciding what to do in our immediate environment, "if it feels right, it is right. If it feels wrong, it is wrong." No one knows but us. No one can really understand our emotional and spiritual attachments to our things.

We all benefit from a fresh start. When we clear the clutter, we experience the world and our inner life with greater clarity and vision.

THERE IS NO HEAVEN BUT CLARITY,
NO HELL EXCEPT CONFUSION.

—*Jan Struther*

22

Face Reality

EXPERIENCE NEVER ERRS. ONLY YOUR JUDGMENT
ERRS BY PROMISING ITSELF RESULTS WHICH
YOUR EXPERIMENTS DIDN'T PRODUCE.

—Leonardo da Vinci

When you're facing a hardship, face it. "Great necessities," Abigail Adams wrote in a letter to her husband John Adams on January 19, 1780, "call out great virtues."

When trouble comes, we must practice active virtue. Difficulties are always unwelcome, and we may become agitated and confused. Ten years ago Peter and I were on a national book tour when Peter tripped on the bottom step of a stone staircase in North Carolina. I was in such shock, I couldn't think clearly at first about the extent of the injury and initially was in denial that I had to cancel several months of speaking engagements.

Many of us have difficulty seeing situations as they are. What mothers can give to children is the example and lessons that help them see things as they are. Children will model their parents in everything, especially issues of honesty. Of all the values we want to inculcate, we want to build a consistent belief in the power of truthfulness. When we are realistic, we can do our best with each situation we face.

Throughout our lives we will encounter problems and can practice training ourselves to face the facts as soon as possible and do whatever is required. I spent a memorable last moment with a dear friend dying of cancer in a hospital. She asked me if she was going to make it. "No," I said, "none of us is." The Buddha teaches us to take it all in. The truth that we all suffer in this human life must be accepted. We suffer less when we accept things we can't change, and try, as best as we can with all our strength and courage, to react in a positive, life-sustaining way. If we accept that death is a natural, inevitable reality for every soul on the planet, we can realistically address a health problem by being armed with information. If a loved one is dying, we want to know in order to demonstrate our love and support with no regrets. No matter what happens, we can make any situation better with knowledge. I always want to know; then I'm in a position to improve the situation if possible.

As good mothers know, we're responsible for explaining to our child how things are, not how we wish things to be. Chuang-Tzu calls us to "stay centered by accepting whatever you are doing."

Don't put off taking action. Don't wait for a better time once you've made up your mind what to do. Good mothers have to do their best every day, and this is a tall order. We can't afford the luxury of waiting for the ideal when the real needs to be addressed.

What are some of the hardest situations you've had to face? What are some of the most agonizing choices you've had to make as a mother? I can remember many sleepless nights, tears, and pain when our children were growing up. We can't close our eyes when reality stares us in the face. Children and parents must come to grips with the truth and their responsibilities in times of need or crisis.

Facing reality isn't limited to dealing with outside circumstances. We also have to come to terms with our own shortcomings, struggles, disappointments, missed opportunities, failing health, and discouragement. If we can't face what's going on, we can't make changes that can be helpful, even life-saving.

What are some of the serious issues you have to address? Is there any part of your life that is in crisis? Are there important decisions you've put off that you can do something about today? Whether you have reached a crucial point in your finances, your health, your memory, your eyesight, or your child's health, or are confronting a problem with depression, drug abuse, or sexual abuse, it is best to seek advice from a trusted professional who will be honest with you, in order to move toward improvement and not deterioration of a situation. Continue to be a truth seeker; this is the way to avoid suffering no matter how sad or bad things can be at times. We don't want to think that horrible things will happen to us or to our family, but experience should tell us otherwise.

The eloquent British poet John Keats, who had tuberculosis and knew he was going to die at age twenty-seven, reminds us the value of experience: "Nothing ever becomes real 'til it is experienced—even a proverb is not proverb to you 'til your life has illustrated it." A basic truth that hits home becomes alive. When it does, grapple with it squarely. Reality never lies or cheats or pulls the wool over our eyes. The truth does make us free.

WE DEEM THOSE HAPPY WHO FROM
THE EXPERIENCE OF LIFE HAVE LEARNED TO BEAR ITS
ILLS, WITHOUT BEING OVERCOME BY THEM.

—Juvenal

23

Uncertainty Stimulates Our Search for Meaning

WE ALL LIVE IN SUSPENSE, FROM DAY TO
DAY, FROM HOUR TO HOUR; IN OTHER WORDS,
WE ARE THE HERO OF OUR OWN STORY.

—Mary McCarthy

We tend to think of uncertainty as negative, but paradoxically it can be a powerful force for all that is true, good, and beautiful in our life. Uncertainty, when properly understood, is what gives our life meaning. Few wise people are completely certain about anything. Socrates often said, "I don't know." The Socratic method of seeking the truth by asking questions reveals how uncertainty can be the catalyst for understanding.

We all know people who are opinionated—dead sure they are right when often they are dead wrong. Certainty closes our mind. We stop searching, exploring, and probing for new discoveries. Uncertainty fosters us to strength of mind. Our friend Bishop John Bowen Coburn knew enough to know he didn't know. His motto was: "You Never Know."

There is so much I don't know. There are important issues I'm not sure about. I'm undecided about so many mysteries. When I'm not sure of something, I'm stimulated to learn more. If it is true that we are using only a small part of our brain's potential, our life can become so much richer when we question everything. We need to make an effort to utilize our innate gifts, and we do this by being unsettled. Leo Tolstoy believed that "life consists in penetrating the unknown, and fashioning our actions in accord with the new knowledge."

When we play it too safe, we die a little. In order to soar, we need to embrace as many expectations as possible. Sophocles taught us that "one must learn by doing the thing; for though you think you know it, you have no certainty, until you try."

There is no guarantee that we will succeed at whatever we attempt to do, but we should still fully engage our energies in living in the present because this split-second moment in time is our only certainty; the entire future is uncertain. "No one can confidently say," observed Euripides, "that he will still be living tomorrow." Uncertainty is humbling and also puts fire in my belly: I want to do all I can while I'm alive and able. There are endless possibilities for giving our life value and meaning. "Without a measureless and perpetual uncertainty," Winston Churchill believed, "the drama of human life would be destroyed."

Look into the unknown. Penetrate the mysterious. Bravely and calmly face doubts. Accept and be grateful for your vulnerability. Good mothers know that they never know, but they can be awake and attentive to all the miraculous uncertainties, intensifying their happiness in the great drama we call life. If we had all the answers and knew in advance everything that was going to happen—including how our children were going to turn out—life would be dull.

Not knowing for certain what will happen next keeps us on our toes. Good or bad news comes, and we will never know one second beforehand. We're fortunate to be continuously surprised by life's master plans. This is precisely what gives our lives meaning: we make the very best of every moment we are alive.

THE QUEST FOR CERTAINTY BLOCKS THE SEARCH
FOR MEANING. UNCERTAINTY IS THE VERY CONDITION
TO IMPEL MAN TO UNFOLD HIS POWERS.

—Erich Fromm

24

Home Is Where You Are

A MAN TRAVELS THE WORLD OVER
IN SEARCH OF WHAT HE NEEDS AND
RETURNS HOME TO FIND IT.

—George Moore

Although I never visited exotic lands with my parents, they taught their four children to feel comfortable wherever we were. Home is not a place but a state of consciousness where you feel happy. A good mother knows the importance of having a well-ordered, attractive home as a base for her family, but it is also important not to emphasize housekeeping at the expense of happiness. I've seen many people unable to relax and enjoy themselves at home. The house can become a trap where the mother's work is never done. A good mother is "at home" with herself, comfortable with the moment's happenings and ready to stop work to "come play with me, Mommy."

I was fortunate to travel the world with my Aunt Betty, my sister, and my cousin when I was sixteen, exploring thirteen countries and thirty-three cities in three months. I adored the adventure and loved exploring the exotic differences of the homes we visited. The smells of curry, incense, and flowers, the bright colors of the costumes, and the traditions were dazzling.

I thrive on book and lecture tours, as I'm fascinated by new people and places. There may or may not be anything quite like a home-cooked meal, but I equally love to try a new restaurant and taste the daily specials. It's all great theater to me.

My advice to mothers is: don't settle down. It's not about the home, it's about the happiness. Everyone told Peter and me that we were wasting our time taking our young children on trips to Europe, but when our daughter Brooke was five, she fell in love with France when we spent a month there, going to museums and chateaus, having picnics in vineyards, visiting cities and villages.

When you're comfortable leaving your safe harbor, you enlarge your vision of life and unity through exposure to different cultures. The food, the music, the décor, and the people increase your appetite to live more freely and add new customs, rituals, and celebrations to your own.

On some of our happiest family vacations, we didn't adhere to old traditions by staying home, but we visited places where the point was to be together, have fun, and do no housework. "Command performances," when a holiday invitation is an obligation for guests and hosts alike, puts pressure on everyone. When we visit our grandchildren, Peter and I stay at a nearby inn, taking pressure off our busy daughter to host house guests and giving us a tranquil retreat at night. Also, because our children are blessed with two sets of parents owing to my divorce, we have established a wonderful new kind of holiday when we celebrate special events, but not necessarily on the exact date of a birthday, an anniversary, or an important holiday. Try getting together on a mutually convenient date when you can travel off peak and hang around with everyone in the flow of their daily lives. Rather than fight holiday crowds and weather delays, visit in the spring, when you can sip beer and grill burgers outside, watching the grandchildren jump for joy in the sprinkler.

Wherever your life's journey leads, know that home is wherever you are happy. Open the boundaries and allow yourself and your children to explore the world. When Brooke lived in Paris for a year after graduating from college, a friend asked me if I missed her. My answer was clear. She was exactly where she felt most at home and where she was the happiest. What more can a mother wish than for her children to find the spirit of place away from the limits of their childhood home?

May you feel at home everywhere and be enriched in your explorations. When you do come home, may you bring the world of discovery with you.

THE GREAT OPPORTUNITY IS WHERE
YOU ARE. DO NOT DESPISE YOUR OWN PLACE
AND HOUR. EVERY PLACE IS UNDER THE STARS,
EVERY PLACE IS THE CENTER OF THE WORLD.

—*John Burroughs*

25

Trust Your Feelings: Be True to Your Essence

THE HARDEST VICTORY IS THE VICTORY OVER SELF.

—*Aristotle*

Ever since I can remember, I've trusted my feelings. When I've made mistakes—and I've made my fair share—I made them because I didn't listen to my heart. Some of my best choices were made against all odds, but I trusted myself and was willing to take the consequences. Too often we do what others expect. We try to please people. We do things we think we should do rather than being true to our essence.

My mother was opinionated about religion, politics, and what's what and who's who. I tried to go along with what she expected of me in order not to be punished. But when I got older I was able to think things through for myself with the help of some adults I greatly admired. Mother loved me dearly and wanted only the best for me, but because she was frustrated in her marriage and pressured to raise four children without an emotional and spiritual partner, she was envious of my happiness. It may seem strange that a loving mother could be envious of her daughter, but I felt her envy deeply and was guarded about what I shared with her right up until she was on her deathbed.

Traveling the world with my aunt at sixteen was a defining moment in my development: on that trip I left home, essentially, forever. Aunt Betty, an international social worker, introduced me to many great minds and souls who cared deeply about improving life for everyone on the planet. I began to study comparative religion and became fascinated with history and politics.

Aunt Betty never had children and was free to spend time in exotic places with her nieces, no doubt something my mother would have enjoyed doing, but she was entrenched in her duties as a mother. I often think how different my mother's life would have been if she hadn't met my father, married, and had four children. She was extremely intelligent and curious, and had desires to accomplish things beyond her role of wife and mother that never materialized.

Being a mother is a role. We play our part without even a dress rehearsal. We either raise our children the way we were raised or we do things differently. We learn quickly what a huge commitment it is to raise a child. A mother imparts the nurturing that sets up the child for life. This great gift is our invisible inheritance. Not a day goes by without my thinking about my mother. Had she not fallen in love with my father,

I would not be alive. I want to please her to this day, and she's been dead for almost thirty years.

One of the genius thinkers Aunt Betty led me to is Goethe, the German scientist and writer who urges, "Just trust yourself, then you will know how to live." A friend, the daddy of three adorable children, told me recently that his mother told him, "always trust your gut." When parents help children to think independently and trust their essence, children receive the gift of inner strength. When we dare to be true to ourselves, nothing can overwhelm us.

Good mothers know they are human beings first, mothers second. While it is always a good choice to make children the priority while they are still in the nest, a mother also understands how important it is to pursue her own interests and to give back to society with her unique talents. In my interviews with mothers, the most personally fulfilled set the best example to their children to be strong, contributing adults by their work ethic, thus instilling a deep sense of responsibility and independence.

Karen remembers how her mother, a professor, always had papers in her lap. Karen had a horse, and Janet faithfully drove Karen to the stables every evening before supper and after a long work day. Janet sat in the car correcting her students' papers while Karen did the barn chores. Karen was responsible for feeding and caring for her horse. Good mothers let a child do things for herself to build self-confidence.

My mother was wonderfully smart to let me have my own garden when I was seven. She warned me that she had her own garden and that I was on my own in caring for my plot. I was true to my essence in seeking solitude in my garden. I thrived on time alone to think things through. My mother, rather than saying no because she was too busy, found a way to say yes to my needs without sacrificing her own.

We are all happy in different ways. No one knows exactly how we feel; we must let our intuition guide us. When we feel comfortable with who we are at our core, we may become aware of how differently we think and feel from our mothers. We, in turn, will observe how different our children are from us, and what a glorious privilege it is to observe their unique ways of self-expression.

Let us all cultivate pure self-awareness as we wear different hats in life—the more varied, the better, making us of greater service to others. Trust your feelings and always be true to the best that's in you, for this is your essential nature.

SELF-REVERENCE, SELF-KNOWLEDGE, SELF-CONTROL—
THESE THREE ALONE LEAD TO SOVEREIGN POWER.

—Alfred, Lord Tennyson

26

Be Prepared to Live!

MAN IS BORN TO LIVE, NOT TO PREPARE FOR
LIFE. LIFE ITSELF, THE PHENOMENON OF LIFE,
THE GIFT OF LIFE, IS SO BREATHTAKINGLY SERIOUS!

—Boris Pasternak

What is more serious and more exhilarating than to live a beautiful, happy life, thriving and getting the most joy out of each day? Who are the people in your life who really know how to live? Think of your mentors and heroes, the bigger-than-life people you know or knew. Who are the people who love life fully? What are some of the things they love? What do they do to maintain their passion?

I had many interior design clients who put their life on hold until all the details were taken care of—but the domestic demands never end, and often are met at the expense of enjoying time with those we love.

Sophocles reminded us that "wonders are many on earth, and the greatest of these are humans."

Endless preparation for living robs us of the richness of our loving interactions with others. Aristotle understood that women, for example, can never be as happy as men because they have too many domestic responsibilities. There is a lot of truth to this. We want to have a cheerful, charming, colorful home environment for our family and friends, but this environment has a way of taking over. Jane Austen asked the key question: "Why not seize the pleasure at once? How often is happiness destroyed by preparation, foolish preparation!"

Charles, a successful interior designer from Atlanta, Georgia, recommends we take ourself out to lunch. Alone, we are to analyze who we are and how we choose to live, what we really want to do, and what we do not wish to do. When are you going to start doing what you like to do? Where do you want to go in this life? Charles feels that when we undergo this self-analysis, we stand tall.

"Find someone who is fifty years older than you and listen to what they say," Charles suggests. Learn foresight from their wise hindsight. Get going and stop talking about it. Don't be afraid to make a mistake. Keep your eye on the road, but be willing to take a detour. Enjoy the ride. Charles, a talented artist, took his own advice and gave up his interior design work to paint full time. William James aptly summed up what's most important: "Life, more life, a larger, richer, more satisfying life."

No one can instruct us how best to live our lives; we have to figure out for ourselves what brings us our greatest satisfaction and pleasure. When you define how you want to live, you get to the heart of your personal happiness. We suffer when we try to fit in and conform. "You must have passion to meet this strange thing called life," the Indian spiritual writer Jiddu Krishnamurti teaches, "and you cannot have passion, intense feeling, if you are mesmerized by society, by custom." We don't owe anyone a piece of our life against our wishes. It is our right and our responsibility to to choose what is right for us.

This day is yours to live! Every moment you are experiencing something important. Good mothers know each new day can be full of wonder, beauty, and joy. The poet Emily Dickinson exclaimed, "To live is so startling it leaves little time for anything else." There is so much beauty to absorb and appreciate, so much to learn, so many interesting people to see and places to go, it is hard to decide just what to do that will be the most satisfying from moment to moment. Life, lived beautifully, is intoxicating with endless options for expression and fulfillment.

You are living the life you are meant to live when you feel this sense of sheer rapture at the feeling of being alive. The more we love life in all its dimensions, the greater our love of others. When Peter and I left New York City, we put favorite possessions in storage. We thought we would miss them, but we find we have more time to live! Studies have proven that objects do not bring us happiness; experiences do. When we don't drag the past around, we're free to see the beauty of whatever we're doing. When a child or grandchild invites us to come play, we drop what we're doing and have fun. Who could ask for anything more?

This moment is the best and *only* time to fully, joyously live! Commit yourself to thrive, to plunge into your aliveness, to revel in the intensity of now. Rather than spend life preparing for future happiness, live now, and let today be the best day you've ever lived, so far.

THE GREAT AND GLORIOUS MASTERPIECE
IS TO KNOW HOW TO LIVE.

—*Montaigne*

27

Value Your Self-Worth

AS IS OUR CONFIDENCE, SO IS OUR CAPACITY.

—*William Hazlitt*

We are all one with the universe, and we all have a Self. The Self is our total being, our individuality, including our moral conduct. I capitalize Self because we should always try to live up to our highest, lightest, brightest best Self. We all have work to do on this unique Self. We are the only person on the planet we can attempt to enlighten.

When you value your Self-worth, others are not a threat to you. You are not in competition with others but want to build on your own gifts and talents. Being overly critical of ourselves is detrimental. If we don't believe in our Self, who will? We need to cultivate trust and faith in the person we choose to be.

We dislike in others what we don't love in ourselves. In order to be worthy of our higher Self, we should embrace our dark and unenlightened side, accepting the base animal nature within. We can't change and improve ourselves until we accept ourselves just as we are.

What are your strengths? What are your innate gifts? What are your weaknesses? What things are difficult for you? Are you a natural with foreign languages, or a whiz in math? Are you full of grace, ease, and dignity in social situations? On a scale from 1 to 10, with 10 being the best, how would you rate your Self-confidence?

Write down some of your positive qualities, things you're proud of and would like to be known for. Write down some of your negative qualities. Consider all the benefits others gain from you. Are you content? Do you approve of who you are and what you stand for? Do you love life and affirm your Self-worth? When you do, you are in a position to find ways to serve others.

I disagree with those who teach that we are not worthy "to gather up the crumbs." When we live up to our inner gifts, we are kinder, more gentle and loving to others. Kind people have high Self-esteem and are always generous-spirited, quick with a compliment, never judgmental, and meet life's challenges boldly.

No one but you will ever truly understand your complex inner world. Don't look around at what others are doing. Studies prove that comparing what we have with others who have more makes us envious and discontented. When, however, we show loving-kindness toward our Self, we share life-affirming energy with others. There is a direct relationship between valuing ourselves and treating others with the respect and dignity they deserve.

Below are some qualities of Self for us to ponder. Some are extremely positive, and some are less so. Many, such as "Self-effacing," can be positive or negative, depending on the degree. As you ponder these qualities of Self, think about these traits you are most proud of in yourself, and what areas you can focus on improving. And remember the wise words of the Swiss psychiatrist Erich Fromm: "Only the person who has faith in himself is able to be faithful to others."

Key Qualities of Self-Worth

Self-taught	Self-sufficient	Self-restraining
Self-reliant	Self-searching	Self-assured
Self-controlled	Self-starting	Self-possessed
Self-denying	Self-confident	Self-less
Self-determining	Self-motivated	Self-loving
Self-disciplined	Self-sacrificing	Self-made
Self-effacing	Self-correcting	Self-actualized
Self-esteeming	Self-discovering	Self-aware
Self-respecting	Self-examining	Self-developed
Self-expressive	Self-protecting	Self-supporting
Self-preserving	Self-sustaining	

I CARE NOT WHAT OTHERS THINK OF WHAT I DO, BUT
I CARE VERY MUCH ABOUT WHAT I THINK OF WHAT I DO.

—*Theodore Roosevelt*

28

We Stumble on Happiness

One cannot forecast the conditions that
will make happiness; one only stumbles upon
them by chance, in a lucky hour, at the world's
end somewhere, and holds fast to the days,
as to fortune or fame.

—Willa Cather

The social psychologist Daniel Gilbert is known as Professor Happiness. A professor of psychology at Harvard University, he directs a laboratory studying human happiness. His book *Stumbling on Happiness* vividly brings to life the latest research about the uniquely human ability to imagine the future.

Gilbert brilliantly explains why we understand so little about "the people we are about to become." Americans have been looking for happiness in all the wrong places, and we have a distorted notion about what will make us happy. Mothers, you'd better sit down. We've been told a story. Many people are duped into thinking they will be happy if they have children. Yet in a study of 900 mothers in Dallas, Texas, most said they'd rather clean the house than spend time with their children! At night when the rambunctious darlings are tucked into bed, the mother relaxes, sips a glass of wine with her dinner, and tells friends that her children are the joy of her life. For some, this is true even during the nonstop chaos of their children's daily demands. For others, enough is enough; they need a break. When children are good they are adorable, but when they are bad, they are horrid. Not every mother has the temperament to devote all her time to the every wish and whim of her growing children.

Professor Gilbert tells us about two huge myths. First, there is the myth that women should have children. We have been brainwashed into wanting children, he teaches, in order to keep the human race alive. If you believe in your heart and soul you were put on this earth to be a mother, then you are richly blessed. The second myth we have bought into is that we should slavishly work to earn money, the more the better, spending time in the workplace at the expense of being with our family. Professor Gilbert cuts to the chase: we need some money as a tool in order to have memorably wonderful experiences. But once we have enough money, more will not make us more happy.

I have seen the money myth enacted repeatedly in my interior design clients who neglected spending time with their children in order to "provide for them." The more they chased after money, the greedier they became for one more deal, one more business opportunity, one more business trip, all at the expense of nurturing, loving relationships with their families. They gave material objects to their children in place of their presence. "You aren't worth my time" is the message their children received. "We think money will bring lots of happiness for a long time," Gilbert writes, "and actually it bring a little happiness for a short time." The new car, boat, or gadget becomes old. Objects don't bring as much happiness as experiences we share with family and friends.

In an interview, Gilbert observed, "Few of us can accurately gauge how we will feel tomorrow or next week . . . Another factor that makes it difficult to forecast our future happiness is that most of us are rationalizers." We have amazing resilience: we "reframe" negative events; we adapt. Our inordinate ability to adapt and rationalize can lead us to think that the next new gadget, vacation, or achievement will be the one that brings true satisfaction. The new watch keeps good time, but we're bored with it; a newer one is now desired. We look forward to tomorrow's fun event and postpone joy today in order to achieve it. We keep throwing the ball of happiness ahead of ourselves—just out of reach.

The happier we are now, the better equipped we are to be happy tomorrow because we have trained our mind, heart, and soul in this healthy way. We will be as happy as we choose to be. True happiness is accumulative and internal; we carry it with us into whatever the future may bring. Precisely because we are phenomenally adaptable, when we want to be happy, we will find our own way.

YOUR IMAGINATION IS YOUR PREVIEW
OF LIFE'S COMING ATTRACTIONS.

—*Albert Einstein*

29

Watch Your Attitude

THE GREATEST PART OF OUR HAPPINESS
OR MISERY DEPENDS ON OUR DISPOSITIONS
AND NOT ON OUR CIRCUMSTANCES.

—*Martha Washington*

In my book *Choosing Happiness*, I wrote that 50 percent of our happiness potential is genetic and 50 percent is environmental. This has been proven repeatedly in research on the brain. Our attitude is a key element in our overall well-being and fitness to cope and thrive in the situations life thrusts us into. Evaluate your mental attitude without judgment. What are your characteristic reactions to circumstances? Do you have a temper, or excessive irritability or sensitivity? "Anger," Benjamin Franklin believed, "is never without reason, but seldom with a good one." What is your usual attitude when you wake up? When you read bad news, does it tend to throw you? Do you fight the weather? What conditions bring you inner peace?

We change ourselves from within through mindful awareness of our attitude. If we have an attitude of gratitude and abundance, our receptive disposition will help us face difficulties, overcome obstacles, and withstand opposing forces.

The poet Maya Angelou teaches, "If you don't like something, change it. If you can't change it, change your attitude; don't complain." Peter and I had an unusually harrowing travel experience several years ago. When we finally arrived home, we vowed we wouldn't complain to others about our trip.

But we did. Somehow we let it slip that we'd had delay after delay, cramped seats, horrifically bumpy rides, and canceled flights. The worst part was the anxiety over whether I could meet my lecture commitment. It took several days to get over this experience. No matter how well we try to watch our attitude, we still have work to do to maintain our inner calm.

Good mothers maintain an attitude of positive expectation rather than a fear-based perspective. Many times warning children not to do something leads them to experiment. I learned this the hard way with Alexandra when she was two, warning her not to put a marble up her nose. Before I knew it, she had a marble up her nose. Rather than accusing children ahead of time by lecturing them not to behave negatively, reminding them of all the things they shouldn't do, it is wise to have certain standards of acceptable behavior—do's rather than don'ts—that serve as the family code of honor.

Good mothers don't complain to their children of their burdens and concerns: complaining is always inappropriate because it puts undue pressure on the child. Everything important in life takes hard work. I've been practicing meditation ever since I went around the world in 1959 and observed people meditating. By being quiet I can become mindful of my thoughts and can change my thinking whenever it is not positive and hopeful. Attitude can also be changed from the outside in: according to sports psychologist H. A. Dorfman: "If your body impersonates an attitude long enough, then the mind begins to adopt it."

The ancient philosophers were inspired by the grace and nobility of nature. When we have an attitude of awe at the spectacular beauty nature provides for us daily, we allow the mysteries of the universe to expand our love of life.

The Buddha shared the essential principles of right attitude in the Noble Eightfold Path:

1) *Right View*: believe in the law of cause and effect and do not be deceived by appearances and desires.

2) *Right Intention*: do not be greedy, do not be angry, and do no harmful deed.

3) *Right Speech*: avoid lying words, idle words, abusive words, and deceptiveness.

4) *Right Behavior*: do not destroy any life, nor steal, nor commit adultery.

5) *Right Livelihood*: avoid any life that would bring shame.

6) *Right Effort*: try diligently to do your best.

7) *Right Mindfulness*: maintain a pure and thoughtful mind.

8) *Right Concentration*: keep the mind right and tranquil for its concentration and seek to realize the mind's pure essence.

The British historian and essayist Thomas Carlyle taught us a key lesson about attitude: "The block of granite which was an obstacle in the pathway of the weak, becomes a stepping-stone in the pathway of the strong." I love this image and want to cultivate the right attitude regardless of what happens. Join me on this quest to live in an attitude of gratitude and love, an attitude that will make all the difference.

WE DON'T SEE THINGS AS THEY ARE,
WE SEE THINGS AS WE ARE.

—*Anaïs Nin*

30

A Room of Your Own

WITHOUT LEAVING MY HOUSE
I KNOW THE WHOLE UNIVERSE.

—Lao-Tzu

I've always found a place where I can enjoy being alone. As a young girl I had my garden or the hayloft. Even best friends need time apart. Everyone needs a place to retreat to, a room of their own.

Good mothers know they need a place where they can go to collect their thoughts, not to be constantly interrupted. A mother makes sure her child has a desk, good reading light, and ample storage. A mother, too, needs her own place where her things are in order, safe from other people's messes. You don't have to be a mother to need your own space, but I believe a mother needs a room of her own more than she'll ever know.

When your room is set up, you can walk in and quickly begin whatever you choose to accomplish. If you don't have your things in order, ready to go, you require time and effort to set everything up, and busy mothers don't have the luxury of extra time. You must value yourself enough to insist on your own private space. No matter how good your concentration is, the kitchen table is not a proper place for your work. Just as an artist has a studio, you need to escape into a private world in order to engage in solitude and replenish your Self. You have important work to do. Go to your private retreat daily, as a pleasant meditation. This place contains your unique energy. It is yours, off limits to others. Unless you make this perfectly clear, you can count on being invaded.

Your room is not a shared space, but a sacred place that is peaceful and expansive. For mothers, private space is a huge treat and a necessity for their sense of balance. Mothers can't be on call all the time. They need some interests that have nothing to do with what their children want them to do. The more isolated your room, the better. When you're out of sight, soon you'll be out of mind. If you're seen, you'll be interrupted. Look for space in the attic, over the garage, or in the laundry room, or convert a guest room.

One imaginative woman who loves to garden uses a corner of the toolshed for her own space. A mother who lives on a farm created a room of her own in the horse barn. In a small apartment, be imaginative. Even if you simply screen off a section of your bedroom that is yours and yours alone, you will be grateful. One mother designated the living room off limits to her twin daughters and set up her desk space inside an armoire.

What do you want to do in this room of your own? The great good news is you don't have to tell anyone what you intend to do in this space.

Begin by considering it a place to meditate and study. Some of you are writers, others are artists. Many women have their own home business. A friend has a bedroom where she hand-paints small love boxes. A mother may want a study where she can read and write. Claim your space and make it work for you. We don't want to merely get by and be good mothers. We want to thrive and be good people. Maybe the secret is to have some private space, and a room of your own. There will not be a day when you won't be grateful you have a room of your own where your personal objects and projects await to inspire you.

Make an appointment to go to your room regularly. I begin my day doing a one-flower meditation in my Zen writing room. Just knowing I'm able to spend some uninterrupted hours studying and writing makes me love my room completely. I can write anywhere—in bed, at a desk, on an airplane, on a terrace. I've even done a fair amount of writing on an ironing board if a hotel doesn't have a desk in front of a window. But wherever I am, I need silence and no interruption. The ideal solution is not to be in sight. Mothers should not have to go to the bathroom to be alone.

A room of your own is a necessity, not a luxury. Here you listen to your Self, your senses awaken, and you feel grateful for your life. Good mothers know they need a room with a door to close. This sacred space is only about you—a calm, safe harbor for your soul.

CONTEMPLATION IS THE ONLY PROVEN
WAY OF CHANGING HUMAN BEHAVIOR
RADICALLY AND PERMANENTLY.

—*Aldous Huxley*

31

Uplift Your Spirit-Energy

WE CANNOT CURE THE WORLD OF SORROWS,
BUT WE CAN CHOOSE TO LIVE IN JOY.

—*Joseph Campbell*

"Ch'i" is the Chinese word used to describe the unique energy that inhabits each of us. It is the spirit or animating force that is felt wherever a person moves. This distinct energetic atmosphere is sensed by others. Sometimes people dismiss this powerful presence, but as the Buddha knew, "When you enter a room you carry a fragrance with you." Some people see colors surrounding a person's head; others feel the positive energy.

I call this phenomenon spirit-energy. Who are the people you know who have an abundance of this powerful energy? People with strong spirit-energy make us feel good in their presence and inspire our best.

Because of their energetic vivacity, they are lively and courageous, and invigorate our lives. They actively focus on what is good and teach us how to participate in the sorrows of the world in a joyful consciousness. Anything we want to do we can do when we enhance our spirit-energy. The loss of spirit-energy can be devastating, and we should continuously remind ourselves how critically important it is to maintain and sustain this vital inner force.

What are the conditions when you feel your spirit-energy is most potent? How do you uplift this inner strength? Good mothers can't run on empty. When their energy is deflated, everyone suffers. It is inappropriate for a mother to expose negative spirit-energy to her child. The damage is far-reaching. No one can raise someone else's vigor. This is up to us.

To help you heal and bounce back as quickly as possible, I suggest you make a list of what tools you bring into play when the wind is abruptly knocked out of you. When your energy is at its best, what are the things you love to do? Where are you? Who are you with? You will grow to understand that these uplifting activities are essential to your well-being. No matter how busy you are, there are certain things you should commit to fitting into your day. I've shared my list below.

A List of What Uplifts Me

- *Spending time with people who have great spirit-energy*
- *Studying Aristotle*
- *Arranging flowers*
- *Walking on a beach*

- *Watching a sunrise or a sunset*
- *Enjoying a delicious meal with a glass of wine*
- *Meditating on and contemplating the great mysteries*
- *Being with my daughters and grandchildren*
- *Hanging out with friends of excellence*
- *Writing*
- *Swimming in the ocean*
- *Being anywhere with Peter*
- *Traveling*
- *Going to museums*
- *Spending time in nature*
- *Sitting in the sunshine*
- *Tying ribbons on presents*
- *Walking around beautiful gardens*
- *Spending time with children*
- *Being with my family*
- *Splurging on truffles in pasta*
- *Writing with a favorite fountain pen*
- *Being kissed by Peter*
- *Giving a genuine compliment*
- *Wearing clear colors*

A List of What Uplifts *You* (for example)

- *Baking*
- *Walking the dog*

- *Gardening*
- *Writing poetry*
- *Going to the movies*
- *Cooking*
- *Entertaining*
- *Decorating*
- *Studying world history*
- *Going to lectures*
- *Praying*
- *Sailing*
- *Playing golf*
- *Having house guests*
- *Going to the library*
- *Painting*
- *Going on bike trips*

Every day, do something that elevates your spirit-energy. As your energy increases, you become lighter and brighter and will bring cheer and hope to all those blessed to be in your presence.

REJOICE IN THE THINGS THAT ARE PRESENT.

—*Montaigne*

32

Share the Piece of Cake

GIVING IS THE HIGHEST EXPRESSION OF POTENCY. IN
THE VERY ACT OF GIVING, I EXPERIENCE MY STRENGTH,
MY WEALTH, MY POWER . . . I EXPERIENCE MYSELF AS
OVERFLOWING, SPENDING, ALIVE, HENCE AS JOYOUS.

—*Erich Fromm*

I read a story in a book about Buddhism of a woman who had invited a friend for coffee. She realized at the last minute that she had only one piece of cake. What was she to do? She absolutely loved this chocolate cake. It wouldn't be possible for her not to have one last final taste. For a fleeting second she had an urge to eat the cake and offer cookies with the coffee. Thankfully she made the right choice and shared the piece of cake.

Because we are social animals, we are happiest when we spend time with friends and family. When there's good company, good conversation, and good food, we are nourished in important ways beyond our body's benefits.

Whenever we share something positive, we spread joy. My love of black truffles is well known among my family and friends. When Peter and I flew to the South of France last January, we visited our dear friend, Roger Mühl. The last meal we shared in his house was a bowl of spaghetti topped with a huge mound of local black truffles. Roger excused himself from the living room to go shave the truffles. When I walked into the kitchen on the way to the dining room I saw a pale apple green plate with scalloped edges heaped with truffles. The scent and sight were intoxicating. The dining experience was ambrosia.

At the airport a few days later I bought a jar of truffles to bring home. Some friends were delighted to share them, and we agreed to enjoy them with scrambled eggs at breakfast. Talk about loaves and fishes—this tiny jar of five truffles was more than enough for the five of us. Each of us shared our personal truffle stories, mine going back to 1963 in Siena, Italy, where I ate truffles that were broiled in olive oil, served with freshly baked bread and a glass of local wine. We had many laughs and shared more than the delicious truffles. We have two truffles left in our little jar, and we're debating whether to begin a magical day sharing them at breakfast or toss them into a bowl of spaghetti. The whole point is to share what we have and create lasting memories.

When we share a piece of cake we eat half the calories. When we share a sandwich, we have room to share a dessert. When something tastes superb, we like to offer a bite to someone. The more you give, the more pleasure you share.

Good mothers are great models for their children when they teach sharing through example. They know how to stretch meals if their children want to invite friends over for the night. We always feel so good when we're generous and thoughtful. Whether we share a smile, a cup of tea, or a seat on a crowded bus, we receive in equal measure or more than we gave. Julian of Norwich, a fourteenth-century mystic, understood that "a cheerful giver does not count the cost of what he gives. His heart is set on pleasing and cheering him to whom the gift is given."

Whether you share the piece of cake with a child, a neighbor, a friend, or a stranger, you will feel enriched by your spontaneous kindness. When we give from our heart and expect nothing in return, we are abundantly blessed. We're able to have our cake and eat it, too!

To be a complete person is to be
a part of others, and share a part of them.

—Elliot Richardson

33

Tenacity Promotes Happiness

YOU HAVE TO PARTICIPATE RELENTLESSLY IN THE
MANIFESTATIONS OF YOUR OWN BLESSINGS. AND ONCE YOU
HAVE ACHIEVED A STATE OF HAPPINESS, YOU MUST NEVER
BECOME LAX ABOUT MAINTAINING IT, YOU MUST MAKE A
MIGHTY EFFORT TO KEEP SWIMMING UPWARD INTO THAT
HAPPINESS FOREVER, TO STAY AFLOAT ON TOP OF IT.

—Elisabeth Gilbert

One of my character traits that has yielded extraordinary rewards is my tenacity. I hold firmly to my dreams, and when I want something badly enough, I don't give up. I'll stick with something to the end if I think it is the right thing to do. I've had many failures and setbacks, but I've also enjoyed great happiness knowing I did my best in each situation. My friend Mary Ann raised her two daughters to be strong women, encouraging the pursuit of their dreams: "As young children Michelle and Melanie swam a mile for charity. It may have taken them a long time, but the plaque in their bedroom rang true: 'You only fail if you stop trying.'"

As a young tennis player I very much wanted to play in a tournament in Florida over the Christmas holiday. How I pulled this off I'll never know, but my parents drove my brothers, sister, and myself from Westport, Connecticut, to Florida. I played in this amazing event and took lessons with Doris Hart, a player I idolized. She taught me a drop shot called "the heartbreaker": you put so much spin on the ball that it bounces across the net onto your opponent's side and bounces back into your court.

When something happens, I give my all to trying to solve the situation, and when I've done everything I can, I face reality and move on. This tenacious spirit can get me in trouble because I'm often determined to work things out against great odds. I remember having some difficulty with a stepchild and felt quite upset things were not working out. Peter sat me down, held my hand, and told me to relax. "Don't take any credit and don't take any blame." Emerson said, "A hero is no braver than an ordinary man, but he is brave five minutes longer." My tendency is to go the extra mile, but there are times when this isn't appropriate and backing off a bit and relaxing is the wise choice. And there are other times when backing off would be tragic.

The now well-documented story of my publisher turning down the initial manuscript for *Choosing Happiness* is an excellent example of my tenacity. I was told it was uneditable and unpublishable. I cried and felt great frustration but would not accept no. I begged to be heard, and ended up writing an entirely different book because I wouldn't stop until my book was published. I intuitively felt that happiness was something my reader had to think about on a daily basis. Doctors and scientists were studying and writing about pathology and misery, and happiness had been ignored. When I feel I'm onto something I am persistent, and when I'm determined I'm often able to be persuasive.

Louis Pasteur has some sage advice: "Let me tell you a secret that led me to my goal: my strength lies solely in my tenacity." My favorite opponent on the court was Billie Jean King. She once said, "Champions take responsibility. When the ball is coming over the net, you can be sure I want the ball." Our happiness is a result of our tenacity as we squarely accept our struggles and create many of our triumphs.

Good mothers often have to resolve situations that are difficult, unpleasant, and often seem overwhelming. But most problems will not go away on their own. Rather than ask "Why me?," we are called upon to show our stripes.

There have been many overwhelming events in my life. But I've always been able to make the best of what I had to work with, and I've learned that we all have a reservoir of inner strength we can depend on whenever the going gets tough. The greater the need, the greater our strength and courage.

Helen Keller, who was blind and deaf, fascinates me in her powerful example of hope and tenacity. Her remarkable teacher Anne Sullivan let us in on the secret: "People seldom see the halting and painful steps by which the most insignificant success is achieved." And her amazing student believed, "We can do anything we want to do if we stick to it long enough." Often, we exceed expectations.

When Alexandra, my first child, wasn't accepted at a private day school two blocks from our apartment, at first I resigned myself to accepting another equally good school. But at the eleventh hour, I knew I had to follow my heart. I asked to have a meeting with the headmaster, and I pleaded with him to pull up an extra chair for my daughter. I said, "She will make the school proud." Alexandra was accepted, and, indeed, she made the school proud as an active, vital member of their community.

Stay focused. Try not to get distracted. If we are persistent, often things will become clear to us. Thomas Edison knew firsthand that "many of life's failures are men who did not realize how close they were to success when they gave up."

Where there is a will, I've always found, there is a way, even if it is often hidden from view.

GIVING UP IS THE ULTIMATE TRAGEDY.

—*Robert J. Donovan*

34

Character Is More Than Good Habits

TO ENJOY THE THINGS WE OUGHT AND TO
HATE THE THINGS WE OUGHT HAS THE GREATEST
BEARING ON EXCELLENCE OF CHARACTER.

—*Aristotle*

Character takes a lifetime to acquire. A good mother models it for her child. If a parent has bad character, the child is at a huge disadvantage.

The qualities of good character include honesty, gratitude, unbiased compassion, loving-kindness, thoughtfulness, decency, loyalty, generosity, empathy, gentleness, and love. If we wish to be respected, we must exemplify self-respect through strong character. People of strong character can ask a lot of others because they ask a great deal of themselves. The more excellent someone's ethical code of behavior, the greater their chances of finding inner peace, contentment, and a meaningful, satisfying life.

Good habits are essential to building character but are not in themselves the active virtues necessary for living the good life. Good habits work from the outside in: you see a weakness in yourself—you are sloppy—but, with effort, you can become neat and orderly. Or you see you need to lose weight, and, as a result, develop good eating habits. Good habits are patterns of behavior and are involved with your own self-interest, whereas character is a quality of mind, heart, and soul that originates within and spreads outward in all directions, benefiting all living souls.

We always know in our soul when we are living with integrity and authenticity. The American psychologist and philosopher William James mused, "I have often thought that the best way to define a man's character would be to seek out the particular mental or moral attitude in which, when it came up him, he felt himself most deeply and intensely active and alive. At such moments there is a voice inside which speaks and says: 'This is the real me!'"

When much is given, much is expected, and when a mother sets a good example to her child of our obligation to give back to others for the great gift of our life and our privileges, she teaches her child how to become a strong resource to others. This is the greatest inheritance we can give our children and grandchildren.

The Soviet writer, dissident, and Nobel Prize winner Aleksandr Solzhenitsyn said at a Harvard commencement address in 1978: "The human soul longs for things higher, warmer, and purer than those offered by today's mass living habits." This wise belief is more true today than ever. There are so many dishonest people running loose in politics, in religion, and in the financial world, it is most important to value the true principles that make us free.

WATCH YOUR THOUGHTS; THEY BECOME WORDS.
WATCH YOUR WORDS; THEY BECOME ACTIONS.
WATCH YOUR ACTIONS; THEY BECOME HABITS.
WATCH YOUR HABITS; THEY BECOME CHARACTER.
WATCH YOUR CHARACTER; IT BECOMES YOUR DESTINY.

—*Frank Outlaw*

35

Quality Living in Every Chapter of Life

I HAVE BEEN THROUGH A LOT AND HAVE SUFFERED A GREAT
DEAL. BUT I HAVE HAD LOTS OF HAPPY MOMENTS, AS WELL.
EVERY MOMENT ONE LIVES IS DIFFERENT FROM THE OTHER.
THE GOOD, THE BAD, HARDSHIP, THE JOY, THE TRAGEDY, LOVE,
AND HAPPINESS ARE ALL INTERWOVEN INTO ONE SINGLE,
INDESCRIBABLE WHOLE THAT IS CALLED LIFE. YOU CANNOT
SEPARATE THE GOOD FROM THE BAD. AND PERHAPS THERE IS
NO NEED TO DO SO, EITHER.

—Jacqueline Kennedy Onassis

A life well lived is all we can hope for, and when we seek excellence in
every chapter of our lives, chances are we will live a life of great quality. If

we drag our old, out-of-date former life into the present and expect our future to be bright, we'll be disappointed. High-quality living requires making choices that are right for you in every stage. How can you live the best-quality life, moment to moment? How can you move ahead with confidence, grace, and joy?

I learned a vitally important lesson one day when I was a young conscientious mother. As was my habit, after dropping Alexandra and Brooke off at school, I dashed to my nearby office and worked nonstop until I picked them up at school. Once home, I made egg salad sandwiches, using a cookie cutter to make them into heart shapes. Standing in the kitchen I nibbled on the scraps, and then I proudly presented both girls with colorful plates of these adorable tea sandwiches, garnished with parsley and cherry tomatoes. Alexandra, age five, inquired, "Mommy, where's your sandwich?"

Oops. I forgot I was at the banquet. I quickly made myself a sandwich, garnished my plate, sat down, and participated in a happy luncheon celebration. Some of my favorite childhood memories were of family meals. I appreciate how busy families are, and eating together is impossible at times, but it is something that gives our lives quality. It doesn't matter how simple the meal, as long as you're "at table" as a family. Thomas Jefferson wrote that he'd "rather be shut up in a very modest cottage, with my books, my family, and a few old friends, dining on simple bacon, and letting the world roll on as it liked, than to occupy the most splendid post . . ." I'm grateful Peter and I made it a priority to eat breakfast and dinner with our children on a fairly regular basis. Saturday lunch was a treat when we'd go to a restaurant until Alexandra and Brooke were older and preferred to be with their friends. These family meals were part of our quality living. When that tradition no longer worked well, we started a new chapter and found other ways to be together as a family.

When we make small rituals of our eating, sleeping, and bathing, we elevate our daily life into quality moments. When we want our experiences to have great meaning, we should ask how we can improve the moment for ourselves and others.

My favorite artist and treasured friend Roger Mühl is a shining example of this principle. When Roger's wife, Line, was too ill to go downstairs the last few months of her life, he set up a sweetly intimate dining room next door to their bedroom, where they dined in style right up until their last supper together. Candles, flowers, wine, delicious food, and devotion were theirs in those treasured hours.

When we make our lives sublime, we lift up the lives of everyone around us. I want to live the art spirit. I want to love purely. I want to make our home safe and happy. I hope that my commitment to living a quality life every day in every way will be useful to others, known and unknown. Good mothers know that a life lived with quality is the highest achievement and the greatest blessing we give to our children and the world.

QUALITY IS NOT AN ACT. IT IS A HABIT.

—Aristotle

36

Challenge Yourself

CIVILIZATIONS, I BELIEVE, COME TO BIRTH AND PROCEED
TO GROW BY SUCCESSFULLY RESPONDING TO CHALLENGES.
THEY BREAK DOWN AND GO TO PIECES IF AND WHEN A
CHALLENGE CONFRONTS THEM WHICH THEY FAIL TO MEET.

—Arnold Toynbee

I went to New York City to study design in 1959. After being a designer for fifty years, I needed to move on to make fuller use of my abilities and resources. I wanted to challenge myself to stretch in new directions.

Life calls forth the full use of our potential. You are the only person you can improve. There are things only you can do. No one else can express what is uniquely yours. The dancer and choreographer Mikhail Baryshnikov wrote, "I do not try to dance better than anyone else. I only try to dance better than myself."

A Buddhist principle is that you should act always as if the future of the universe depends on what you do, while laughing at yourself for thinking that whatever you do makes any difference. I don't think any of us really knows how much we can mean to others. Perhaps something we say or do makes a difference, or we extend some small act of kindness; whatever it is, I have witnessed the enormous impact one human life can make on another by challenging ourselves to do our best under all circumstances.

Unless we're passionate about challenging ourselves, we will make millions of excuses why we don't have time to read, study, paint, or write. Last year, I read, 53 percent of Americans surveyed by the National Endowment for the Arts hadn't read a book in the previous year. Dare to summon the necessary action to stimulate your mind every day you're alive. Beyond doing what is expected of us, we have to raise the bar and become better today than we were yesterday. We have to remember our brilliance.

Ask what good you can do today and make no excuses. Set a timer and engage in some form of active virtue for one hour. Find another hour and get back at it. In every hour of the day, be all you are capable of becoming. A Hindu proverb says, The true nobility is in being superior to your previous self.

There are a lot of things that are unworthy of our serious attention; at the end of the day, they don't add up to much. For every hour you spend on your household, spend equal time on your mental work. When we neglect our higher self, our soul suffers.

We alone can use our powers to create something wonderful that would not exist without our effort. William James urged us to challenge ourselves: "Compared to what we ought to be, we are only half awake. We are making use of only a small part of our physical and mental resources." Maria Montessori, the Italian physician and educator, developed a method of educating children that stresses development of the child's own initiative. Good mothers know they have more free time to do their own work when they raise a self-reliant child.

If you want to do something new, try it. Remember Shakespeare's advice, "Action is eloquence." Aim high. Dream big. Do whatever you can to produce a body of work that will not die. Aristotle believed that "happiness is an expression of the soul in considered actions."

Welcome challenges and live an intensely exciting, vigorous life of effort and great meaning. Seize this moment to push yourself and experience the exhilaration of self-expression: this is you at your best. And then, keep on keeping on.

I DON'T WAIT FOR MOODS. YOU ACCOMPLISH
NOTHING IF YOU DO THAT. YOUR MIND MUST
KNOW IT HAS GOT TO GET DOWN TO EARTH.

—*Pearl S. Buck*

37

Identify What Is in Your Control

A MOTHER IS NEITHER COCKY NOR PROUD,
BECAUSE SHE KNOWS THE SCHOOL PRINCIPAL MAY
CALL AT ANY MINUTE TO REPORT THAT HER CHILD HAS JUST
DRIVEN A MOTORCYCLE THROUGH THE GYMNASIUM.

—*Mary Kay Blakley*

You can always control yourself. No one can take your self-control away without your permission. You exercise authority and influence over one person on the planet: yourself. You have the power to manage your emotions, not those of others, as good mothers know.

How many times are we mortified by our young children's behavior when we're in public, and how many times do you think our children are embarrassed by their parent's carrying-on? Good mothers learn that they can't control everything their children think, feel, and do, but no matter how chaotic things are around you, you can make a conscious choice to control your emotions.

From early childhood to dying and death, much of our behavior is about wanting to control the outcome of things. We find it rewarding to make things happen, to master new skills, attain goals, and see the results of our labors. We enjoy teaching a child to read, and it is exciting when the training wheels go off the bike. Even when things are not in our control, we want to be in charge of the uncontrollable. (I do acknowledge that there are poor women all over the world who may have no control over where they live, how they spend their time and money, and even what they eat. When we do have some control we are most fortunate.) Consider some of the things that are in your control:

- *Your mood*
- *Your spirit*
- *What time you get up in the morning*
- *What you do with your time, energy, and money*
- *Where you live*
- *How you live*
- *What you value*
- *How you love*
- *What you care about*
- *What you focus on; what you want and choose to do*
- *The food you eat; what you drink*
- *The colors you surround yourself with*

- *The people you let into your inner circle*
- *How you reach out to others in service*
- *Your sense of appreciation*
- *Your understanding of the nature of reality*
- *Being a good mother*

Now consider what is not in your control. You cannot control another human being. It's grandiose to think you can; we have a difficult enough time controlling ourselves. We can't control the weather or when the sun rises and sets, but there is a wealth of ways to affirmatively respond to the aspects of our lives that are our responsibility to handle well. We can't control what happens, but we can make creative use of all the happenings, and when we don't fight the inevitable, we let life happen and we are happy.

There is a Zen saying I think of often: Sitting quietly, doing nothing, spring comes and the grass grows by itself. This knowledge of the rhythms of nature is comforting; we can ease up a bit and not think everything is up to us.

There are times in our lives when we're forced, by outside circumstances, to give up control. One of the most painful recent times for Peter and me was at a rehabilitation health care center following Peter's knee surgery. One day you have control of your life and, in a blink of an eye, you are robbed of all control. Rather than deciding what you want, suddenly you are told what to do, when, and how to do it. The atmosphere was depressing. I was told that only hospice nurses were allowed to spend the night. But I did spend the night—in an uncomfortable chair. There was no tub or shower in the bathroom, no long distance calls allowed, and no exit. I was in shock, and so was Peter, who is least happy when he is held in limbo.

Even such events as airline delays are maddening in the way they rob us of control and a sense of order. For me, the most difficult pill to swallow is the one I don't want but that is forced upon me by some authority figure. When my personal freedom is taken from me and I lose all control, then I am left to control my inner world and hope my resources are adequate for the occasion.

I guess, ultimately, the only thing we can count on and control is the quality of our love—and our ability to be a good sport! We can always maintain control over our attitude. It informs everything we think and do. By controlling our attitude, we gain huge control over our lives, because we are choosing to honor our commitment to our higher self.

SOME THINGS . . . ARRIVE ON THEIR OWN MYSTERIOUS
HOUR, ON THEIR OWN TERMS AND NOT YOURS, TO
BE SEIZED OR RELINQUISHED FOREVER.

—*Gail Godwin*

38

Continuously Reorganize Priorities

ONE NEVER NOTICES WHAT HAS
BEEN DONE; ONE CAN ONLY SEE
WHAT REMAINS TO BE DONE.

—Marie Curie

Every new day has its own personality. Variety gives us vitality and zest. Routine robs us of enthusiasm. I've never been bored because I always have years' worth of interesting things I want to accomplish and squeeze into the precious waking hours of my days. Each day has different logistics, and some things we do take precedence over others because of what we value.

When mothers are organized and the children's affairs are in order, they are free to make intelligent use of their time. I've discovered that women, especially mothers, tend to have a difficult time doing what they really want to do because they spend their day doing things for others or what they feel they should do. The meals get cooked, the laundry gets washed, folded, and put away, rooms are tidied up, errands are done—and, once again, the mother's day has slipped through her fingers. Everyone and everything else takes priority.

Good mothers always put their children first when safety or health are at stake, but it is otherwise inappropriate for a mother to devote all her energies to her child. The great good news is that when a mother takes good care of her child she will actually have more free time to pursue her interests because her child will thrive in an easy-going, loving environment.

The way to give yourself the gift of free time every day is to be flexible and open to shuffling things around depending on the weather, your mood, your energy, and the demands of others. Most people resist this free-form way of managing their daily lives, but there will never be enough time if you routinely put your interests last. There will be interruptions and requests, and others will waste *your* time with *their* priorities.

After the family's basic needs are met, put yourself first. Do what only you can do, something you're passionate about, something that you have to do or else you will feel anxious and frustrated. Make a list of what these things are. One mother wants to write a book about early child-hood development. Another mother loves to make handmade greeting cards at the kitchen table every morning after the children get on the school bus. The secret is to give yourself the best part of the day, the big-gest chunk of uninterrupted time when you have those glorious blank white spaces in your calendar. Set a kitchen timer for sixty minutes. Listen to the tick-tick of the seconds. Be aware of the precious gift you've given yourself.

Go one hour without checking your e-mails or talking on your cell phone. If one hour is all the time you can give yourself, make a pact that you will set that time aside every day, seven days a week. You will be amazed how much you can accomplish in seven hours a week, four weeks a month, twelve months of the year.

Where there is a will there will be a way, but only when you're able to continuously reorganize priorities. When I was working full time as an interior decorator while raising two lively daughters, I had a burning desire to write a decorating book. I set the alarm for 5 A.M. and put in two productive quiet hours every morning. I became so enthralled I found myself going to a coffee shop to write after walking the girls to school, before I went to my office. I avoided making lunch dates and instead walked over to the Museum of Modern Art to sit in the garden and write. After Alexandra and Brooke were in bed I wrote, often staying up late. Nothing could stop me, and after seven years of effort and focus, my first book was published.

Make no excuses. Whenever we say we don't have time, we are kidding ourselves. One woman complained that her husband demands a meticulously clean house. I suggested he clean it himself or that he hire a housekeeper. Last year I was overwhelmed with work that forced me to prioritize. No fooling around. I set a timer and logged in my hours.

Now that my children are grown, my number one priority is Peter. I'd drop anything, however, to be with and to be helpful to our family. Now there is plenty of time for me to do my work and still remain flexible. If you're not prepared for an important meeting, it is far better to postpone it than to waste other people's time.

A good mother knows how to continuously reorganize her priorities in order to fulfill herself as she assumes the awesome responsibility and privilege of raising good children.

THIS IS THE TRUE JOY IN LIFE,
THE BEING USED FOR A PURPOSE RECOGNIZED
BY YOURSELF AS A MIGHTY ONE . . .

—George Bernard Shaw

39

Give Your Children Their Own Space

THE MORE PEOPLE HAVE STUDIED DIFFERENT METHODS
OF BRINGING UP CHILDREN THE MORE THEY HAVE COME
TO THE CONCLUSION THAT WHAT GOOD MOTHERS AND
FATHERS INSTINCTIVELY FEEL LIKE DOING FOR
THEIR BABIES IS THE BEST AFTER ALL.

—Benjamin Spock

Our child is not our possession. Children are with us for a relatively brief but crucially formative period. Nine months or so in the womb and approximately eighteen years in the nest is the basic time frame we have to be their guides, teachers, cheerleaders, and their greatest influence.

During this time we're on call to help our children develop their characters, gifts, talents, and personalities to the best of our ability and re-sources. We love our children and want the best for them, and feel proud of their every achievement, but we must be on guard not to interfere. Good mothers don't meddle or intrude in their children's affairs. They know their children need their own space. Good mothers don't smother, depriving their child of exploring and building confidence in their own judgment and ability. At the same time, mothers don't neglect any appropriate opportunity to help.

What a fine line mothers must walk. They can't be too demanding that their children excel in every area, but they should encourage a child's interests and talents. They're there to support but not to push. Parents are not meant to shape their children in their own image. Each human life is unique, without equal or equivalent. A child has different genes, a different temperament, and what's theirs is not ours. We are very different from our children. We should never begrudge their free spirit. Children are literally in their own world, a world that is very different from ours.

Sadly, when a mother is not self-fulfilled, she tries to live through her children. Ann, a mother I interviewed, admitted how awkward it was to have her mother, Sonja, tell her every sordid detail about her marriage to Ann's father and how jealous she was of Ann. Imagine the burden this placed on Ann as she tried to develop her own self and life. Eventually, when Ann married, her husband helped her to set strict boundaries in order for Sonja not to interfere in their lives and in the way they chose to raise their children.

Lao-Tzu taught an essential lesson: "If I keep from meddling with people, they take care of themselves; if I keep from commanding people, they behave themselves; if I keep from preaching at people, they improve themselves; if I keep from imposing on people, they become themselves."

Our children are in the process of becoming. Let them be. Give them space to breathe, to feel their spirits soar, to let their personalities develop. They will grow up, as we well know, in spite of us. Freedom that goes both ways benefits both parent and child. When we love deeply, there is no concept of possession.

CHILDREN REQUIRE GUIDANCE AND
SYMPATHY FAR MORE THAN INSTRUCTION.

—*Anne Sullivan*

40

What's Most Important to You?

YOU DO WHAT YOU HAVE TO DO BECAUSE
YOU FEEL THAT IT IS IMPORTANT, BECAUSE IT IS
HELPING PEOPLE AND IT IS MAKING
A DIFFERENCE IN YOUR LIFE.

—*Deepak Chopra*

At a talk in West Virginia, I inquired, "How many of you think about your own happiness every day?" A few people raised their hands. When I inquired how many think about their children's and grandchildren's happiness, they all raised their hands.

We have to value our own happiness with our whole heart. No one can give from a hollow heart. Everything becomes a drain. When we place our happiness first, we're in a position to be an excellent role model, a guide our child can mirror.

We shouldn't seek happiness in order to be a better mother or parent. We should want to be happy in order to find our best ways of living well as we try to serve others, including our children. You make a difference in all the lives you touch. It's important to strive be the person you believe you are meant to be. You are unique. Life is limited. You have only a certain number of years. You have to decide what you are going to do in your particular circumstances. What makes you happy? What makes you fulfilled? In addition to your partner and your children, who and what makes you rejoice?

Remember, you have the power to cause either joy or sadness in others. Your children are living their lives under your amazingly powerful influence. When I was young and my mother was upset, I felt I was to blame. If a mother is unhappy, there is a tendency for her to be envious of her child's happiness. She may feel her child achieved happiness at her expense. No child deserves this burden.

Happiness, broadly described, is doing what feels good, what we take pleasure in, what is good for us and, in turn, what is good for others. There is great happiness in being true to your ideal self. Happy people wish to do no harm. If you love your life, you will find many different outlets to be of service to others. Life reciprocates. There is a mutual interchange. What good we give returns to us. The mother who does what is right tends to have a reciprocal relationship with her child.

Eric Butterworth, the beloved minister of Unity Center in New York City, wisely understood that "this is what work is, or should be—a celebration of yourself." Raising a child is hard work. What's most important to me is to know I am doing my best—to fulfill myself, to be happy, and to enrich the lives of my children, family, friends, and the world. We can only spread happiness and love from a happy, loving heart. If each of us found our own way to be happy, I believe the world could unite in love.

ONE CANNOT HAVE PLEASURE WITHOUT GIVING IT.

—Hermann Hesse

41

Gentle Strength: Your Great Virtue

THE GENTLE MIND BY GENTLE DEEDS IS KNOWN.

—Edmund Spenser

No mother is perfect any more than any child is perfect, but some mothers are perfectly wonderful. My husband Peter's mother, Miriam, was as good a mother as was humanly possible. Miriam had gentle strength. Her positive influence was profound. Miriam was brave, strong-willed, disciplined, and confidently feminine. Emerson could have been describing Peter's mother when he wrote, "Self-command is the main elegance." With authority and grace, she raised four children in New York City during the Great Depression.

Miriam called a family council meeting in the family library one

Friday in 1933 to announce that there would be no flower delivery until further notice. Every Friday afternoon, fresh flowers had arrived at the apartment, and Miriam joyfully arranged colorful, fragrant bouquets. Peter was eleven in 1933, the depth of the Depression. He vividly recalls this particular day as being symbolic of the overall pressures a mother of four was under in such a difficult economic time. Because of her gentle strength, Miriam was able to perservere with dignity.

Peter remembers Miriam was always in touch with all four children, but never interfered. Peter was the baby. When the older siblings were at school, he enjoyed his mother's undivided attention. She took him everywhere, including an art studio where she took painting lessons. She also designed her own jewelry, knitted, and sewed. She loved to make holiday decorations and cheerfully had her children join in on her artistic projects, together with everyone else including visiting friends.

When Peter was very young his mother took him to see a retired sea captain who spent his retirement years carving wood objects. She urged him to carve mallard ducks, and once he was persuaded, they were so graceful she had to almost beg him to part with them. Once home, Miriam painted those wooden birds, and they were glued to a wall of the library flying freely against a soft sky blue.

Gentle strength is win-win for mother and child. Miriam participated in all the family activities. A superb athlete, she loved swimming in the Atlantic Ocean on the New Jersey coast. A favorite summer recreation was daily picnics on the beach. Her celebratory nature became ingrained in Peter: the first summer we were married, Peter and I rented a sweet house on Orange Street in Nantucket, and we headed for the beach every day to have fun in the sea and sand—always with a picnic.

Miriam believed in persuasion, not swatting. She was always gentle and civilized. She loved to recline in a chaise longue in the master bedroom before going out in the evening for a party. She'd lie down for a little nap to restore herself before an evening out.

Her gentle strength encouraged her husband, George, whom she adored. He had a seat on the stock market and was under inordinate stress throughout the Depression. Miriam had some of her own money and was exceedingly generous with what little she had. She was always evenhanded with the funds she gave the children.

When I asked Peter to tell me a most happy, memorable moment with his mother, not surprisingly, his memory was about the ocean, Miriam's favorite athletic joy. At a small swimming club on Long Island bay, at age four and a half, young Peter was told by his mother, "Today you are going to jump off the dock, and I'm going to catch you." She was down below, treading water, arms up, reaching for her frightened son. The water was way over their heads. "I will give you an ice cream soda, Peter. Jump." Peter jumped into her arms. He was so happy he jumped several more times before getting out of the cold water, teeth chattering. After wrapping him in a huge beach towel, Peter's mother gave him a favorite treat called a Manhattan—half coffee ice cream, half chocolate ice cream, and soda water he sipped through a straw.

As busy as she was as a full-time mother, Miriam made a point of powdering her nose and putting on lipstick every late afternoon when the doorman rang the buzzer alerting her that her husband was in the elevator. Miriam took her apron off and greeted George at the door.

Grace notes such as these are available to us even under stress. When my friend Dana's mother was in hospice care, weak as she was, she asked

Dana to help her find a brush she kept in a bedside drawer, and she brushed her hair in anticipation of her husband's visit. She was always happiest when her husband was with her. My mentor, Eleanor McMillan Brown, kept a compact in a drawer in her drawing room, and she'd powder her nose before guests entered the room. Perhaps these were ways these women acknowledged themselves, taking a moment to become centered.

What can mothers do to cultivate gentle strength? What can all of us do to live with this gracefulness, exposing our softness while being the rock, the anchor, the support? We can all take a page from Miriam's book. There are so many gentle ways to show your care and love. Her kind of strength was to give a little pat, a hug, or rub the back of a child who needed a little extra support and attention. My daughters loved me to rub their feet when they were upset. When we demonstrate our soft side, we show our strength.

LOVE IS SWIFT, SINCERE, PIOUS,
PLEASANT, GENTLE, STRONG, PATIENT,
FAITHFUL, PRUDENT, LONG-SUFFERING.

—*Thomas à Kempis*

42

Children Don't Own You

CAN THERE BE A LOVE WHICH DOES NOT
MAKE DEMANDS ON ITS OBJECT?

—Confucius

Children shouldn't own their parents any more than parents should feel entitled to own their children. An important shift happens when a child matures: parents and children evolve into a relationship more guided by the Golden Rule than by the children's needs. There comes a time when there should be mutual give and take.

After all the years you've spent being there for your children, savor this time when everything doesn't revolve around them. Take all the space you need. Take the trip. Suppose you've never seen the Great Wall. If not now, when? Barring exceptional circumstances, your children have what they need and should no longer be the center of their parents' universe.

Sometimes children want to have their cake and eat it, too: while they want to spread their wings and fly away, they still want their parents to support their lifestyle if they can't manage to do it on their own. Too many parents go to the grave with their child feeling entitled to demand whatever they can get away with. Nothing, absolutely nothing, should be automatic. Children shouldn't feel they "deserve it." Parents should feel free to donate art to a favorite museum, money to a library they loved, or give gifts to friends near and far instead of to their children.

Parent-child relationships should not be centered around money but around the giving and receiving of love. When we genuinely care about each other's happiness, we will act accordingly. Children must grow up, and it is childish to want everything. The richest inheritance is the legacy of character, a desire to be of service, shared memories, generational friendships, wonderful stories, a work ethic, and the greatest bequest of all: your love. Try to love each other purely without judging, and when appropriate, forgive each other.

THE CHILDREN NOW LOVE LUXURY, THEY HAVE BAD MANNERS, CONTEMPT FOR AUTHORITY, THEY SHOW DISRESPECT FOR ELDERS AND LOVE CHATTER IN PLACE OF EXERCISE. CHILDREN ARE NOW TYRANTS, NOT THE SERVANTS OF THEIR HOUSEHOLDS. THEY NO LONGER RISE WHEN ELDERS ENTER THE ROOM. THEY CONTRADICT THEIR PARENTS, CHATTER BEFORE COMPANY, GOBBLE UP DAINTIES AT THE TABLE, CROSS THEIR LEGS, AND TYRANNIZE OVER THEIR TEACHERS.

—*Socrates*

43

Celebrate Freedom of Spirit

IF YOU WANT TO FOLLOW ME TO FREEDOM,
BE PREPARED TO SWIM UPSTREAM,
AGAINST THE RIVER OF CONDITIONING.

—*The Buddha*

In my career as an interior designer I saw many beautiful houses but few happy homes. Most of the wives were playing traditional roles that were huge traps. The real estate, cars, boats, planes, and objects all required maintenance. The role of hostess left little time to celebrate any freedom of spirit. I saw that all the trappings that could and should make someone happy can make someone sick, sad, and in some cases mad.

We will never feel our life is successful unless we live each day in our own particular, often peculiar way. We are, in a real sense, private property. Each of us is without an equal. We are literally unparalleled.

Being free to be *you* requires that you have the courage of your convictions. Rollo May believes that "courage is required not only in a person's occasional crucial decision for his own freedom, but in the little hour-to-hour decisions which place the bricks in the structure of his building of himself into a person who acts with freedom and responsibility."

I have learned to be a free thinker. So much of what I've been taught and gone along with I now do not believe to be true for me. I am not trapped and won't let myself be a victim. I do not assume traditional gender roles. When something doesn't work out or is no longer appropriate or fun, I do something else. I choose not to be frazzled, frustrated, and flustered. I care deeply about being me and protecting my freedom of spirit.

Let your spirit fly! Have opinions, become something, express your real self. Go places, learn more about you, come back thinking fresh ideas and skip, whistle, laugh at life's foibles, and laugh at yourself. This shaping of self is your job. Finding your essence is a thrilling adventure that goes on forever, one discovery after another.

President John Kennedy believed that "conformity is the jailer of freedom and the enemy of growth." A favorite author, Nikos Kazantzakis, the creator of the most adorable, lively spirited creature Zorba in *Zorba the Greek*, urges us to "die every day. Be born again every day. Deny everything you have every day. The superior virtue is not to be free but to fight for freedom." I do this every single day I live, inspired by Zorba.

Try not to crush your spirit by being too logical or efficient. My friend Betsy has a strong work ethic but when the surf's up, she's there to greet the big waves. She finds a way to celebrate her spirit freely when the moment presents itself.

What are some of the things you love about yourself that are over the top?

Peter, for example, has never *built* a small fire but makes bonfires! His love of water reveals itself daily in his long showers—and sink time takes at least half an hour. When my friend Toni, in a hurry to put dinner on the table, asked her husband Donald "to do something with those potatoes," Donald started to juggle them. They both had a good chuckle.

What are some of your quirks? What's considered unusual about you? Be proud of your idiosyncrasies; without them you'll have a taupe personality—and as many friends know, I can't cope with taupe!

What will people laugh about when remembering you after you're dead? I hope they'll say you were a character. Below are some of my quirks; have fun making a list of yours.

A List of Some of My Quirks

- *I don't like to drive, so I don't drive.*
- *I discovered early in my life that I do not enjoy typing. My father made me take a typing class in high school so I could be a secretary to a boss. Just because I can type doesn't mean I should. I'm the boss! Or would like to be.*
- *I write my books with a favorite fountain pen on French stationery.*
- *I am not interested in dealing with technology. I do not use a computer because it doesn't bring me pleasure.*
- *I'm passionate about bright, clear, clean, saturated colors and wear them throughout the year, rain or shine.*
- *I have pens and ink cartridges in every conceivable color; they make*

me smile. I use bright colored note paper that is not considered "professional."

- *Formality makes me uncomfortable. When I'm in pretentious situations I feel like a bull in a china shop. I prefer elbows on the kitchen table to rigid rituals.*
- *I'd go to great distances to eat a black truffle . . . or two . . . or more.*
- *I love to work hard.*
- *I prefer to eat my meals with chopsticks rather than with a heavy fork.*
- *I'm so passionate about the beauty, color, and fragrance of flowers I would lose my freedom of spirit if I couldn't feast my soul on them every day, whenever I can.*
- *Whenever we travel we make no plans in advance other than booking our hotel in order to celebrate our freedom.*
- *Peter and I spend every moment of our lives together and never feel we can get enough of each other. "But not for lunch" does not apply to us.*
- *I like my gray hair and looking my age, but not acting my age.*
- *I haven't weighed myself or been weighed for more than twenty years.*

I was astonished when I read the Roman historian Tacitus, who laments, "It is the rare fortune of these days that a man may think what he likes and say what he thinks." How much progress have we made in these thousands of years? For far too many woman around the world have not made nearly enough progress. How free are we? What do we fear? What and who prevents us from celebrating our freedom of spirit? You can't afford to wait until everyone who doesn't approve of your freedom of spirit dies. The Buddha teaches, "You are your own Master." His Holiness the Dalai Lama reminds us that you go through the "Main Gate" without your guru. The beloved journalist Walter Cronkite observed, "There is no such thing as a little freedom. Either you are all free, or you are not free."

Look deeply and mindfully at your true nature and take charge of your life now.

DEPEND UPON IT THAT THE
LOVER OF FREEDOM WILL BE FREE.

—Edmund Burke

44

Dare to Embrace Enlightenment

The important thing is not to stop questioning.
Curiosity has its own reason for existing.
One cannot help but be in awe when he contemplates
the mysteries of eternity, of life, of the marvelous
structure of reality. It is enough if one tries
merely to comprehend a little of this mystery
every day. Never lose a holy curiosity.

—Albert Einstein

The greatest gift you can give your child is your own enlightenment. Your goal of attaining enlightenment helps others. This truth may seem paradoxical, but I believe it to be our wisest choice. The mother-child relationship requires someone who dares to embrace enlightenment. No one on earth is in a better position to be a shining example to her child, instilling spiritual and intellectual insights, than a mother. A mother should be an ideal example to her child of what the good life looks like close up. A mother's moral excellence, her sense of decency and honor, her intellectual and spiritual commitment to what is true, beautiful, and good, are more powerful influences on a child than mere knowledge and information.

Lao-Tzu understood that the true sage teaches without words. We teach best by example, our active virtue. If you want to raise a good child, you have to be a good person. If you want your child to be happy, *you* must be happy. If you want your child to discover the thrill of learning, you must show your enthusiasm for study. Mothers have to be exemplary because children by nature are sponges, absorbing everything.

How can we move onward and upward in our lives, experiencing real transcendence? Imagine a flight of stairs. We dare to embrace enlightenment by standing exactly where we are on the staircase, seeing, as Emerson pointed out, "stairs before us, which we seem to have ascended, there are stairs above us, many a one, which go upward and out of sight." Faith keeps us climbing toward the light. The top is invisible, the climb steep; but when we commit ourselves to moving toward the eternal mystery, we receive timeless moments of clarity and glimpses of the unity that is our potential.

I believe human beings are basically good, but the perfection of our true nature is often buried by negative feelings and actions that make us suffer instead of becoming happy. If a mother spends all her energies in trying to perfect her child, she is not taking responsibility for her own self-mastery. Once a woman takes responsibility for her own transformation, she becomes a positive channel to her child.

How can we strengthen our mind to cultivate a more positive attitude? What can a mother do to become more dependably patient when she could so easily be at her wits' end? How can she remain loving when faced with negative circumstances beyond her control?

One of my favorite practices on my quest to embrace enlightenment is the one flower meditation. I have practiced this contemplation for as long as I can remember. I simply sit quietly and look into the face of one flower until I become one with the flower. There is no elaborate ritual. But inevitably this private, simple ceremony leads me farther on my path toward the serenity and clarity I am forever seeking. If you can see with fresh eyes the beauty of one flower, perhaps this may be the first step toward embracing enlightenment. In that flower we see firsthand the universe we are an intricate part of; we submit to and live in harmony with nature rather than trying to dominate it, and we empty ourselves in order to become full and spread loving-kindness in a world in great need of beauty, clarity, inner peace, and happiness.

We transform the world from the bottom up. First we find meaning in our lives in order to help others, many of whom are suffering. Then, with each person spreading light and joy, something sublime happens. The light spreads and shines in dark places, and happiness becomes our nature. Reach high, spread your wings wide. Dig deeply into your consciousness.

You don't have to try to be a good mother. Being a good human being supports and sustains all good works. Every sacrifice you make will become a blessing to you and countless unknown others.

Embrace enlightenment and claim the freedom and power to become the messenger of the good life, the life well lived, the happy life of personal transformation and excellence in service to others.

Lift off and soar and rise, and rise
toward the confident and the good and
the beautiful. Rise toward the compassionate
and the gentle and the caring.

—*Desmond Tutu*

45

Searching Questions About Mothers

NOT MANY OF US REALIZE HOW IMPORTANT
QUESTIONS ARE IN OUR LIVES, BUT THIS IS THE WAY WE
BECOME PERSONALLY ENLIGHTENED.

—Peter Megargee Brown

I believe, as Socrates taught us, that we best seek the truth by asking questions. In that spirit, this essay asks questions about your mother and about you. This is, of course, not a test; I hope you will use these questions to deepen your insights about yourself and your mother. You may want to have a pad of paper handy for notes and insights.

Questions About Mothers

- *What do you love the most about your mother?*
- *Do you believe your mother has good values?*
- *Is your mother good at managing money?*
- *Does your mother have a strong work ethic?*
- *Do you think of your mother as being altruistic?*
- *Does your mother expect a great deal from you in proportion to what she expects from herself?*
- *Who are the people in your mother's life who did the most to encourage her self-actualization?*
- *Was your mother patient with you when you were growing up?*
- *Do you feel that sometimes your mother tries to interfere with your life?*
- *Do you ever feel an obligation toward your mother that is, in reality, a burden to you?*
- *Do you ever feel your mother made unnecessary sacrifices for you?*
- *Do you think your mother pays enough thought to her own needs and happiness, or does she have a tendency to think of others' happiness first?*
- *Does your mother have a spiritual practice that she pursues daily?*
- *Does your mother try too hard to look younger than she is?*
- *Does your mother approve of your love partner?*
- *Is your mother happy?*
- *Do you consider your mother to be wise?*
- *When your mother is upset, does she have a tendency to blame you or others?*

- *What are your mother's finest characteristics?*
- *Where are some of the places you've explored with your mother?*
- *What is (was) your mother's relationship with her mother?*
- *What is your mother doing to empower herself?*
- *What are you most proud of about your mother?*
- *What has your mother had to overcome?*
- *What is your earliest memory of being alone with your mother?*
- *What are some of the habits, customs, and ceremonies you inherited from your mother?*
- *Do you consider your mother open-minded?*
- *Is your mother generally positive?*
- *What were some of your mother's biggest causes for concern when you were growing up?*
- *Did you always know you were an important priority for your mother?*
- *What are some of the values your mother instilled in you when you were young?*
- *What are some of your favorite things to do together?*
- *What are some of your mother's interests that excite her passion?*
- *Have there been certain defining life events that have brought you closer?*
- *Do you feel that if you needed your mother, she would drop everything and come help you?*
- *What are some of the times when your mother has been most vulnerable?*
- *Do you ever write your mother a love letter to remind her how much you love and appreciate her?*

- *Does your mother write you sweet notes to remind you of her unending love?*
- *What does your mother teach you about yourself?*
- *What are the impressions about your mother you most remember from when you were young?*
- *Do you always feel loved by your mother?*
- *What were some of the things you did only with your mother, one on one?*
- *What are your mother's three strongest character traits?*
- *Write down ten words that you believe capture your mother's personality at her best.*
- *Do you feel that your mother respects your privacy?*
- *How does your mother meet challenges?*
- *What is the guiding force in your mother's life?*
- *How often do you feel your mother experiences joy?*
- *Do you consider your mother a good role model?*
- *What important life lessons have you learned from your mother?*
- *Is there a mother figure other than your mother who you love and admire?*
- *How does your mother express her creativity?*
- *Does your mother take good care of herself—mind, body, and spirit?*
- *What are some of the things you look forward to doing with your mother in the years ahead?*
- *If your mother were to die tomorrow, what do you think she would write in a last letter to you?*
- *What is your fondest memory of your mother?*

- *If you could spend quality time together, what would you most enjoy doing?*
- *Is there any other mother figure you admire?*
- *When you do certain things that you know would make your mother proud, do you feel closer to her?*
- *Did your mother value personal, lasting happiness?*
- *If you could sit and visit with your mother today, what are some of the questions you would ask her?*
- *What are some of the sentimental objects you have from your mother? Describe them in detail.*
- *When you face a challenge, do you contemplate what your mother would do in the circumstances?*
- *Exactly how did your mother empower herself?*

Questions to You as a Mother

- *Do you treat your children differently from the way you were raised?*
- *Do your children know their own greatness?*
- *What is the most rewarding thing about being a mother?*
- *How did you instill in your child a sense of personal responsibility?*
- *Do you have an opportunity to teach other children besides your own?*
- *Do you take relatively good care of yourself?*
- *On a scale from 1 to 10, what is your natural set point of happiness?*
- *Are you good at delegating? On a scale from 1 to 10, what is your score?*
- *Do you think you have realistic expectations for your child?*
- *Are you a perfectionist?*

- *Do you feel you understand your child?*
- *No matter how hard the work, or how demanding your responsibilities, do you always feel nourished by the love you share with your children?*
- *Do you believe you give your child adequate privacy?*
- *On a scale from 1 to 10, how patient are you?*
- *Do you think you generally criticize your child constructively?*
- *How often do you spend undivided time alone together with your child?*
- *Do you have any favorite mother-child rituals?*
- *What are your favorite mother-child rituals?*
- *If your child were to describe you to friends, what would she/he say about you?*
- *What do you like most about being a mother?*
- *How good are you about letting go?*
- *Do you think it's a hard job to be a good mother?*
- *Does your child have some of your personality traits? What are the personality traits your child shares with you?*
- *If your child is young, do you have any plans and goals for yourself after your child is grown up and living an independent life?*
- *How often do you have a good laugh with your child?*
- *What is the most charming thing about your child?*
- *Are you a good listener?*
- *Did you ever do your child's homework? Why?*
- *Do you feel you maintain a healthy balance between spending enough time with your child and spending time alone to study and pursue your own interests?*

- *What is the most important thing you want for your child?*
- *What is the most important thing you want for yourself?*
- *Do you feel being a mother has helped you to be a better, more understanding person?*
- *Do you feel the maintenance of your lifestyle to be stressful and too demanding of your time and attention?*
- *Do you revise your priorities when your life circumstances change?*
- *Do you have a room of your own, off limits to everyone but yourself?*
- *Do you spend time each day working on your personal transformation?*
- *Are you able to look forward and not dwell on past events that you can't change or improve?*
- *Do you feel you are living up to your potential?*
- *What is your idea of time off?*
- *How much do you value your own happiness?*
- *What are your own great strengths you can always count on?*
- *As the years go by, faster and faster, do you feel happier and happier?*

IT IS BETTER TO KNOW SOME OF THE
QUESTIONS THAN ALL OF THE ANSWERS.

—*James Thurber*

Afterword

You and I are on our way, on a path toward enlightenment. The greater our spiritual progress, the more knowledge we gain of our shortcomings. It's most important that we continue our inner work. Celebrate moments of clarity, seek to be guided by pure love, and use your spirit-energy to benefit others.

Good mothers know never to look back at their mistakes, but to embrace the present opportunity to be an active force for good. A mother continues to evolve into her brilliance as she grows in ways to empower herself. As you deepen in knowledge and grow in spiritual values, you gain inner freedom. Motivated to do good and never do harm, you and I become increasingly aware of our huge potential to help ourselves and others in a wide range of ways.

One happy mother can spread great light, not just to her own children but to people of all ages near and far. Together we can elevate the spirit-energy of the universe.

LET
ALEXANDRA STODDARD
INSPIRE YOUR LIFE

978-0-06-128463-2 (paperback)

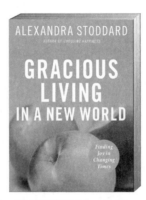

978-0-380-72620-2 (paperback)

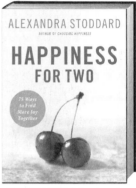

978-0-06-143563-8 (hardcover)

978-0-06-000804-8 (hardcover)

978-0-06-079664-8 (hardcover)

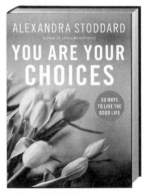

978-0-06-089783-3 (hardcover)

WILLIAM MORROW
An Imprint of HarperCollins*Publishers*

www.harpercollins.com

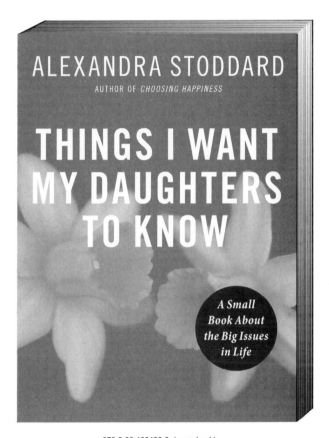

ALEXANDRA STODDARD
AUTHOR OF *CHOOSING HAPPINESS*

**THINGS I WANT
MY DAUGHTERS
TO KNOW**

*A Small
Book About
the Big Issues
in Life*

978-0-06-128436-6 (paperback)
978-0-06-059487-9 (hardcover)

"A wealth of advice . . . simple yet so poignant."

—*Southern Women*

**These and other titles by Alexandra Stoddard are
available wherever books are sold, or call 1-800-331-3761 to order.**

WILLIAM MORROW
An Imprint of HarperCollins*Publishers*
www.harpercollins.com